Praise for *Headamentals*

"This is the book every leader needs at some point in their career—especially in those moments of uncertainty. It offers simple, actionable tools to spot self-doubt early and keep you leading with confidence."
NICOLE AYERS, Business Unit Director, General Mills

"*Headamentals* is a phenomenal book for any business leader. I loved the pragmatic exercises and the highly recognizable examples. I can truly state I am a better, more focused, and happier leader having read this book."
MIRANDA PRINS-VISSCHER, CEO, GBfoods Europe

"Business is a team sport. Whether your arena is a boardroom or somewhere else, *Headamentals* is a go-to resource for any team looking to win."
LANDON DONOVAN, legendary US soccer player

"*Headamentals* is an invaluable guide for both new and seasoned executives. It's more than a mindset manual—it's a field guide for clear thinking, decisive action, and purpose-driven leadership. As a first-time CEO, I found it indispensable."
AGNELO FERNANDES, CEO, Cote Hospitality

"For leaders ready to level up, *Headamentals* delivers real insights and actionable strategies. Pick this book up, do the work, and watch yourself soar."
NICOLE ZUBE, Executive Vice President and Chief Human Resources Officer, SpartanNash

"This book is a game-changer for anyone in a leadership role. It's a powerful guide to silencing self-doubt, reclaiming confidence, and leading with clarity and conviction."
AMBER LUSSIER, Director of Resort Marketing, Harrah's Resort Southern California

HEADAMENTALS

HEAD

Suzy Burke PhD
Ryan Berman
Rhett Power

AMENTALS

How Leaders Can Crack Negative Self-Talk

Copyright © 2025 by Suzy Burke, PhD,
Ryan Berman, and Rhett Power

All rights reserved. No part of this book may be reproduced, stored in a retrieval system or transmitted, in any form or by any means, without the prior written consent of the publisher or a license from The Canadian Copyright Licensing Agency (Access Copyright). For a copyright license, visit accesscopyright.ca or call toll free to 1-800-893-5777.

Cataloguing in publication information is
available from Library and Archives Canada.
ISBN 978-1-77458-589-4 (paperback)
ISBN 978-1-77458-590-0 (ebook)

Page Two
pagetwo.com

Page Two™ is a trademark owned by Page Two Strategies Inc., and is used under license by authorized licensees

Cover design by Cameron McKague
Interior design by Peter Cocking
Printed and bound in Canada by Friesens
Distributed in Canada by Raincoast Books
Distributed in the US and internationally by Macmillan

25 26 27 28 29   5 4 3 2 1

headamentals.com

This book is dedicated to you. For it is you who willingly puts in the work to slay the complicated Monster that lives inside your head.

Contents

Preface *1*

Introduction: Head Games *3*

PART ONE **THE PROBLEM: THE MONSTER**

1. Inner Narratives *13*
2. Impostor Syndrome *33*
3. Self-Handicapping *51*
4. Confirmation Bias *65*
5. Experiential Avoidance *71*
6. The Amygdala Hijack *79*
7. Overthinking *93*

PART TWO **THE PROCESS: THE 3-C MAVERICK METHOD**

8. The Cognitive Reframe Game *107*
9. Catch It *117*
10. Confront It *131*
11. Change It *143*

PART THREE	**THE PRACTICE: RETRAIN YOUR BRAIN**	
	12 The Big 5 Monster Archetypes	*157*
	13 Mastering Maverick Habits through Action	*175*
PART FOUR	**THE PLUTONIUM: TEAM-TALK**	
	14 Team-Talk Starts at the Top	*195*
	15 Business Is a Team Sport	*209*
	16 Cognitive Distortions within Teams	*225*
	17 Be the Change	*251*

Conclusion: Celebrate Your Growth *265*

A Word of Caution *267*

Acknowledgments *269*

References *272*

The mind is its own place, and in itself can make a Heaven of Hell, a Hell of Heaven.

JOHN MILTON

Preface

Hear that?
Of course you do.
It's talking to you.
Not even whispering.
How can it be so loud?
Yet, no soul outside your soul can hear it.
Listen closer.
It's doing what it does.
Swaying your thoughts.
Spinning up worries.
Making you feel small.
This is your Monster.
This is what it does.
Your Monster doesn't want you to turn the page.
Your Monster doesn't want you to change.
Your Monster doesn't get a say.

Let's begin.

Be careful what you say to yourself because you are listening.

LISA M. HAYES

Introduction
Head Games

THAT DREAM JOB you've had your eye on has finally opened up. You've put in the time, and you're next in line, but another internal candidate, Paul, is vying for the same position. Worse yet? He is less qualified than you are, and he's only been with the company for two years.

One catch: Paul is quite charismatic. He's proficient at self-promotion and office politics. He's been campaigning for the position by seeking out influencers in the company and highlighting his accomplishments. He has also started spreading rumors about you, suggesting you aren't as well suited for the job as he is.

Deep down, you know you're the best fit for the promotion, but even so, you start to spiral. You find yourself questioning whether Paul's tactics will sway the decision-makers. You're now losing a lot of time worrying about the wrong things. You're known for getting things done, but with your mind elsewhere, your work output is beginning to slip. Your speed to decision slows, and your productivity is starting to suffer.

Ask any corporate leader what their true product is, and the answer should be simple. It's not a widget, a service, or even a breakthrough idea. The true product of any business is productivity.

A leader's mission is to keep people focused, energized, and churning at the speed of modern business, humming on a conveyor belt of professional potency. Wouldn't it be nice if all businesses could maintain this rocket ship pace? But the robots have yet to take over. If they had, this book would look entirely different than the one you find in your hands.

"We the people," in our raw human form, remain complicated creatures, a fact that often leads to, well, complications. The stories we tell ourselves, both fact and fiction, can cause a serious slowdown. The experts call this self-talk. And if we're not careful, the negative tales we tell ourselves will prevent us from forging ahead. So much gets in our way, and so much goes on in our minds, making us less efficient:

- Lack of alignment
- Miscommunication
- Uncertainty
- Need for clarity
- Request of an unreasonable client
- Resignation of a leader
- Frequent pivots that impact your performance
- Politics of someone like Paul

These are some of the fits and starts that cause loss of momentum. Most of the time, this is just stuff that's happening around you at work, but it can sure feel like it's happening to you—which fans the fires of self-talk.

According to the National Science Foundation, the average person has up to sixty thousand thoughts a day, and up to 80 percent of these musings are negative. That's forty-eight thousand negative thoughts every twenty-four hours! To make matters worse, the study also revealed that up to 95 percent of those debilitating thoughts are repetitive. Think about the weight of all that worrying. This inner conundrum happens regularly to the best of us, and it brings out the worst in us.

Stress or pressure to perform at work can usually be attributed to unrealistic targets, inadequate resources, a lack of clarity about the direction of your corporate locomotive, or any combination of these. If we're not careful, we'll spin ourselves out of control. Suddenly, we're strumming up fictitious narratives in our minds, and that product of ours (productivity) is on a self-imposed sabbatical.

This is how negative self-talk blazes through our brains. It's like having Usain Bolt sprinting around in there, breaking records and killing our confidence. This brings us to a point about self-talk we seldom consider. Everyone on your team—including the Pauls of the world—is also battling their own inner Monster, and no one's passing the baton. Indeed, negative self-talk can quickly impact team-talk. And self-doubt can morph toxically into team-doubt.

This is hard enough to handle as an individual, but for those of you in a leadership role, you have the added pressure of ensuring your team is productive. The quietest and quickest killer of a team's confidence is sabotaging self-talk, and the real losers are:

- You
- Your productivity
- Your team
- Your culture
- Your business

We created *Headamentals*—fundamentals for your head—to help you get your head in the game so you and your team can get ahead. As three executives and coaching practitioners who have spent a collective hundred years working with leaders running every type of vertical across the world, from the largest corporations to aspirational start-ups, the authors noticed hard-to-detect self-talk patterns shared by many of the employees, teams, and organizations we interact with.

Specifically, we discovered that the stories you tell yourself get hit back and forth like a tennis ball in your mind. It's a matchup between the "Determined You" who wants to remain confident against a "Derailed You" who spins out. (Thanks a lot, Paul.) Here's how these two voices play out:

Derailed: I know I'm the best-qualified person for the position, but that may not matter. I worry that senior management won't see the political game Paul is playing. Even though I've been a loyal employee who always delivers results, I still may not get the promotion I've earned.

Determined: I know that spending more energy on a situation that's out of my control is a waste of time. If they choose Paul, it says more about the leaders of this organization than it does about me. I've delivered for the company since Day One. Tomorrow, I'll talk with the CEO and share some ideas I plan to explore if I get the promotion.

Will you succumb to the derailed story or embrace the determined story? The choice is yours.

Our Mission: Produce Confident Leaders and Productive Teams

Having been on the front lines consulting or coaching hundreds of leaders and founders over the years, we know that debilitating self-talk affects everyone (including us). We wrote this book to help leaders of all stripes quell the derailed self-talk in their minds. Whether you're leading a well-established team in a global corporation, an agile team in a start-up, or a small-town nonprofit board, your negative self-talk is limiting your success.

Negative self-talk undermines confidence and intensifies the stress that comes with big jobs. Equally important, it impacts a leader's effectiveness because when leaders engage in negative self-talk, they limit their ability to inspire and motivate their teams. They diminish their ability to recognize and act on opportunities for growth and improvement. Negative, derailed self-talk can also lead to a self-fulfilling prophecy, where leaders start to act in ways that affirm their negative beliefs.

By learning how to minimize negative self-talk, leaders and teams can be more productive, maintain a more positive outlook, make better decisions, and function within a more constructive and collaborative work culture.

Our Promise: A Method to Quiet Your Monster

By now, you might have pieced together that we believe negative, derailed self-talk is truly a Monster in your mind. This Monster, when untamed, stomps on your productivity, smashes your creativity, and runs your corporate aspirations straight into the ground.

In the pages ahead, we'll teach you about the inner workings of your Monster: what it likes to feast on, and how it might go about slowing down your decision-making and, ultimately, your progress. We'll share where your self-defeating thoughts come from and help you understand the impact negative self-talk has on your energy, your efforts, and your life.

While this may not be a surprise to you, each of our Monsters affects us differently, gorging on entirely different thoughts and scenarios. In Part One of *Headamentals*, "The Problem," we shine a light on the psychological barriers and human tendencies that lead to Monster-generated negative self-talk. We then dissect six specific manifestations of the hearty "Monster Fuel" many of us consume. If you're the type of person who wants to crack themselves open to discover how you happened, you'll be a fan of Part One. We highly recommend not just absorbing the concepts presented, but actively engaging in the self-reflection exercises woven into each chapter.

In Part Two, "The Process," we'll teach you about another voice in your head that shares space with your Monster—the positive and determined self-talk that we call the "Maverick." We'll teach you our 3-C Maverick Method, a simple-but-not-easy, three-step process you can use to reframe your negative self-talk:

1 Catch It
2 Confront It
3 Change It

You will need to create new habits in order to "Catch, Confront, and Change," and that takes commitment, determination, discipline, and hard work. As part of the process, we'll give you the opportunity to build and incorporate positive mini-narratives in your daily activities. The reflections we ask you to complete and the assessments we provide will serve as strength training for your Maverick muscle so you can be more confident, courageous, and resilient in the face of the challenges and setbacks that are inevitable in any leadership role.

We're confident you'll get there because *Headamentals* is packed with self-guided training exercises and activities to help you cement the insights you've gained.

Part Three, "The Practice," is where you retrain your brain by applying real-life *Headamentals* through scenarios built around the Big 5 Monster Archetypes that show up most often.

Once you've mastered your personal Monster and learned to flex your Maverick muscle, we turn our attention to Part

Four and something we call "The Plutonium," where we share the ultimate multiplier: transformative leadership tools to enhance team-talk for an engaged, optimized, productive, and powerful corporate culture.

Crucially, we're going to help you recover the one thing we all crave and need more of: time. The less time you spend spinning inside your head, the more time you'll have to be productive throughout your day.

Our intention is to provide you with a concise resource to guide you through the messiness of self-talk. This doesn't mean eating positivity pellets for breakfast every morning. It means learning to mentally unhook from the repetitive, harmful stories your Monster feeds you. When you acknowledge what no longer serves you and choose more positive messages for yourself, you will soar, unencumbered.

Let's dive in.

PART ONE

The Problem
The Monster

Inner Narratives

Anybody who has survived his childhood has enough information about life to last him the rest of his days.

FLANNERY O'CONNOR

ANY CHRIS ROCK fans in the house? The sixty-year-old comedian has countless accolades for his work in film, television, and stand-up comedy. Listed as a top five comedian of all time by *Rolling Stone* magazine, Rock transcends the medium with his humor, style, and cut-through-the-butter-with-a-knife brute honesty.

In his 2023 Netflix special, *Selective Outrage*, he brings forward his hilariously slanted observation about how of all the animals on the planet, only humans need slow-cooked, around-the-clock parental supervision from the day they are born. Rock passionately protests from the stage, "You realize, human beings, we have the worst offspring of any animal. We're the only animal in the whole animal kingdom that raises its kids for *eighteen years*. Eighteen years! Every other animal is like two or three days!"

The inner workings and complex wirings of humans are both our blessing and our curse. Let's take a time machine back to the very first seconds of our lives. Remember when you were born? Of course you don't. When you first arrived, you went from nine months of comfortable, quiet darkness to a chaotic flash of screaming, "Hello, world!" From that moment on, you had no choice but to figure life out and began learning at a crazy pace. You discovered that smiling garners hugs and laughter from your caregivers. You picked up on the fact that walking gives you control and freedom. That every action comes with labels, judgments, consequences, praise, or criticism.

You might have enjoyed a childhood full of positive reactions from adults. Maybe your parents told you that you were smart or a good kid. You woke up in the morning with a smile, ready for anything. But most people have mixed memories of growing up. They witnessed difficult relationships, addictions, jobs lost and found, uncertainty, and illness. Good things happened, and bad things too. The stains of life stick with us like an imprint on the mind that never goes away.

When you were a child, life was simpler because there were rules to follow. Even when the rules were unfair, you knew where you stood. You were likely rewarded when you did something positive and punished when you did something wrong. Easy, right?

As you got older, you learned to tell yourself "this is good" or "that's bad." You formed an internal moral compass that (mostly) pointed you in the right direction and corrected you when you stepped out of line. You learned about things like achievement, pride, and confidence, as well as disappointment, fear, and the shame that came when you failed to meet high expectations. You leaned into the behaviors and activities that made you feel good (e.g., learning, sharing, playing, volunteering) and avoided things that made you feel lousy (e.g., flunking a test, or not being invited to a friend's birthday party).

Then you grew up. The training wheels of life were removed, and life became more abstract, stressful, and confusing. You had to face new challenges: getting a job, finding a partner, or moving to a new city. Your inner narratives undoubtedly encouraged you to play a wide-ranging cast of characters.

One day, you're a determined and confident Maverick. You know where you're headed and why. The next day? You're plagued by a derailed Monster. These narratives serve to either deplete us or energize us. The truth is we all have a plethora of competing thoughts running through our minds. It's hard to pinpoint which state you're even in if you aren't thinking about these two alternatives.

Evolutionary Hardwiring

Ever heard the saying "Some patients are just not in a position to be operated on"? It's often used metaphorically, particularly by leaders, and it suggests that not every manager is ready to face significant change or intervention at a given time. Think of a time in your career when you went into a meeting where a big decision needed to be made and, right or wrong, your mind was made up before you even set foot in the room. Your hardwiring would not allow you to be swayed by another person's point of view. You were the patient who couldn't be operated on.

This is all of us from time to time. Our evolutionary makeup does not always serve our best interests.

Ryan Berman spent over five hundred days talking to people who study how we operate. They included Cambridge PhDs, clinical psychologists, and classically trained immunologists. He learned that we're more wired than we realize, less driven by pure emotion and more by intricate circuitry, operating like complex machinery beneath our human exterior. Our standard operating system—our central nervous system—is hardwired to be on the lookout for danger.

This wiring was extremely helpful three hundred thousand years ago when the survival of our species relied on avoiding deadly situations at all costs, like being cornered by a ferocious bear while simply trying to nosh on berries. In a world where tigers and bears could devour you while you slept, staying vigilant, steering clear of rustling bushes, and sleeping in protective groups were useful skills.

Over the course of evolution, dangerous beasts became less of a daily concern, but other dangers took their place: fear of rejection, fear of embarrassment, and fear of shame, to name a few. Instead of warning us about wild animals, well-intentioned parents and peers alerted us to other dangers:

"I don't know, Buddy. That seems too hard for you."

"You're not _____ enough for that."

"You won't be able to succeed in that job once they get to know you."

Modern humans have a different understanding of danger. Environmental and societal variables have tricked us into states of fear and stress that no longer serve the same purpose they once did. Thanks to technology, the world has evolved, but our outdated primal operating systems have not. You may be able to fully participate in that Teams meeting in your self-driving car through your connected earbuds, but if your autonomous vehicle is going nowhere in a sea of traffic, that very same bear-is-chasing-you-for-berries derailed response will cause fireworks in your mind. You'll grow more frustrated by the second sitting in traffic, all because you're more of an antique than you even comprehend.

The previous example isn't the only way our antiquated fight, flight, or freeze brain gets us. Many of us react to uncomfortable conversations, finding new friends, or taking on challenges as if a poisonous snake were about to bite us. This fear exacerbates negative thought patterns. By constantly trying to sidestep everything that might be difficult, we end up avoiding anything that isn't easy and enjoyable.

Your Monster under a Microscope

As Ryan taught us in his book *Return on Courage*, our central nervous system is doing exactly what it's supposed to do: keeping us "safe." That desire for safety manifests through the Monster in your mind. The negative stories it tells you are a constant reminder of all the metaphorical hot stoves you shouldn't touch over the course of your life. But when your Monster runs mission control, you might as well settle into a comfortable suit of Bubble Wrap and a life devoid of optimism. Because when your Monster becomes the primary voice in your head, you're constantly looking for opt-outs instead of the intriguing and experimental all-ins. When you opt out to stay safe, however small the perceived danger may be, you're limiting your potential. Indeed, choosing to stay safe can be highly unsafe.

It makes you wonder: Where exactly do our Monster narratives come from? How did they shape us from the get-go? Was it a parent or caregiver who significantly influenced your self-perception? Was it a tough-as-nails sports coach or music instructor with a "my-way-or-the-highway" mentality? Was it a teacher who seemed to give more attention to others, causing you to feel neglected? Was it a teasing or bullying encounter on a school bus? Was it a reflective moment in the dark you had with yourself just before bed, replaying all of the above in your mind, that caused you to feel depressed, anxious, or sad? Was it simply generational genetics where a parent's pessimism was passed straight down to you?

It takes hard work to understand where your negative self-talk comes from and who you may have to address (and forgive) for planting these destructive stories. Behind every limiting belief you have about yourself is the source of this belief, and it's both essential and insightful to understand where it all started. Yes, this is a therapy moment, and you can't duck the origin story of destructive dialogue.

Negative self-talk comes from a variety of sources, including:

Internalized criticism: If you've been surrounded by people who criticize you or put you down, you may start to believe them. Get these people out of your life now, or at least put your earplugs in when they start ragging on you.

Past experiences: You may internalize past experiences and blow them up into negative beliefs about your self-worth.

Comparison: Constantly comparing yourself to others and feeling like you don't measure up leads to feelings of inadequacy and self-doubt. When you recognize you're doing this, put a stop to it.

Perfectionism: Perfectionists are driven by feelings of never being good enough. When you're mired in self-doubt, remind yourself of Suzy Burke's husband's wise observation: Nobody's perfect.

Trauma: Traumatic experiences lead to feelings of shame, guilt, and self-blame.

Genetics: Some of us are just hardwired to fear spiders, clowns, commitment, or heights. Each of us can be triggered in unique and mysterious ways.

As soon as you spot a moment when self-talk has sent you into a spiral, create the space to have a hard conversation with yourself about what's truly behind the destructive message. And if you can figure out the origin of your self-deprecating thoughts, that's precisely the moment when change can happen.

> **MAVERICK PRO TIP**
>
> Schedule a fifteen-minute calendar meeting with yourself every week to audit what you say to yourself. While this may seem awkward at first, it will help you develop a mechanism to short-circuit your menacing Monster.

When you notice you're speaking to yourself negatively, stop and ask yourself why.

Are you repeating something you heard someone say about you? Are you holding on to some stained moment from your childhood? Do you really believe what you're telling yourself? Do you think belittling yourself will motivate you to work harder? Or are you simply feeling tired? Or hungry? What's this really about?

As Chris Rock reminded us, there's a reason we should live at home with our parents until we're eighteen. It's hard to be a human! And there are many reasons to be wary of those almost two decades' worth of voices that penetrate our minds, forming the "truth, and nothing but." Our inner narratives shape how we talk to ourselves when no one is listening but us.

The voices we adopted, absorbed, and now listen to each day weigh in on just about everything, judging our talents, choices, skills, physical appearance, intentions, and desires. They compare us to our peers and question who we aspire to

None of the repetitive, harmful, degrading narratives you tell yourself truly define you.

be. They demean us into submission. The weight of the positive and negative commentary varies based on the situation, but there is hope because we know two things to be true:

1. None of the repetitive, harmful, degrading narratives you tell yourself truly define you.
2. You can choose to create new, more empowering narratives that will better serve you.

Overcoming the challenge of negative self-talk will enable you to go through your days feeling fulfilled and help you to achieve what you know is possible. But how do you choose which voice to listen to? How do you manifest a new habit that will enable you to hear a truer, more encouraging perspective? Most of all, how do you minimize the time you spend on unproductive ruminations that stem from your past and live in the deep corridors of your brain? Will you succumb to the derailed story your Monster feeds you, or will you embrace the story your determined Maverick offers? The choice is yours.

Headamentals: Short-Circuit Your Autopilot Monster

Let's revisit that critical meeting when you already had your mind made up before you walked in the room. Maybe Paul showed up to the meeting too and you couldn't help but turn the main thing into a brain thing. Perhaps you were so caught up on looking smart or separating your point of view from Paul's that your Monster got the best of you. You start to reflect on why a stubborn version of you showed up—maybe it was because you were passed over in a previous career. Maybe it was never just about this Paul, but about all the Pauls you've worked with before. Whatever it was, this scenario has stuck in your mind, and you can now see how maybe this is more of a *you* problem than a Paul problem.

Take some time to reflect on the origins of your inner narratives and document the messages that have stayed with you about yourself over time. As much as we don't want to make an episode of *This Is Your Life*, you may need to trace those memories—the good, the bad, and the brutal ones—back to your childhood.

Please don't skip this part. If you want to conquer the Monster in your mind and embrace the Maverick, you must do the work, even if it's painful. Remember, we're all flawed and messy. So, give yourself some grace and consider what made you... you. Unpack yourself to figure out how your Monster grew. Once you do, you have a shot at short-circuiting your autopilot self.

What were three of the most frequent *positive* messages you received in the first ten years of your life?

_____

_____

_____

What were three of the most frequent *negative* messages you received in the first ten years of your life?

_____

_____

_____

What were three of the most frequent *positive* messages you received in your teens?

_____

_____

_____

What were three of the most frequent *negative* messages you received in your teens?

_____

_____

_____

What were three of the most frequent *positive* messages you received in your twenties?

_____

_____

_____

What were three of the most frequent *negative* messages you received in your twenties?

_____

_____

_____

What were three of the most frequent *positive* messages you received in your thirties?

_____

_____

_____

What were three of the most frequent *negative* messages you received in your thirties?

_____

_____

_____

What were three of the most frequent *positive* messages you received in your forties and beyond?

_____

_____

_____

What were three of the most frequent *negative* messages you received in your forties and beyond?

_____

_____

_____

How were those questions for you? Did you dig deep and remember something about yourself, positive or negative, that you had buried or forgotten? That mental soil can be compact and hard to penetrate! Yet, it's critical to address what was once compartmentalized or suppressed.

Look at the observations you captured in this exercise. Did you confront the source? Did you uncover a theme? How much are these messages still haunting you or shaping your sense of self-worth?

Your internal narratives articulate and reinforce your thoughts and emotions. They wield a profound influence on your identity and behavior. They can inspire you and keep you secure, or they can stand in the way of what you intuitively know to be true. The encouraging truth is that you're the one who holds the most power over which narratives you heed and how you present yourself to the world.

Two Wolves

There is much to be learned from a well-known parable, "The Tale of Two Wolves." As the story goes,

In a serene forest nestled between towering mountains, an elderly grandfather sat by a crackling fire with his young grandson. The sun cast long shadows through the trees, and the air was replete with the tranquil sounds of nature.

Filled with the wisdom of years gone by, he looked into his grandson's eyes and said, "My child, within each of us, there are two wolves, and they are locked in a ferocious struggle. One wolf lives in harmony with all that is around him. He does not take offense when no offense is intended. He will only fight when it is right to do so and only in the right way. He is filled with serenity, love, empathy, hope, kindness, and generosity.

"But the other wolf is full of anger. He is bathed in jealousy, fear, regret, self-pity, and resentment. He snarls at the world, always ready for a fight. The littlest thing makes him nasty and aggressive. He is always in a bad mood, and he cannot think clearly because his anger is so great.

"It is hard to live with these two wolves inside of me because both are trying to dominate my spirit."

"Which wolf wins?" the grandson asked.

The grandfather responded: "The one you feed."

Take a few minutes to reflect on this. Your Monster is the angry wolf, spewing negativity. Your Maverick is the good wolf, filled with calming empathy.

Now, consider the following questions. Our only request is that you be honest with yourself. Have that internal heart-to-heart, even if it's hard.

Set aside at least twenty minutes to think about the messages your angry wolf is sending you. That angry wolf, whispering (or screaming) in your ear, is your Monster at work. We know twenty minutes may seem like a lot of time, but it's worth capturing what your Monster is saying to you in the space below.

What traits of the good wolf do you embody?

_____

_____

_____

What traits of the angry wolf live within you?

_____

_____

_____

In a typical week, how often does the good wolf prevail?

_____

_____

What enables the good wolf to take the lead?

_____

_____

_____

How often is the angry wolf in charge?

_____

_____

Under what circumstances does the angry wolf surface?

_____

_____

_____

_____

_____

While it may feel like you're the only one struggling to articulate your inner monologue, remember that many people, perhaps even at this very moment, are thinking about these very same brave responses. You're not alone.

From Texas to California, Bruce Pollock built a successful career over four decades managing and growing major market radio stations across the United States. He's had his fair share of ups, downs, and in-betweens over his lengthy career. But one constant he shared with us is that he continually battles negative self-talk. Bruce said, "I had to get over the anger and fear in my head, or I would never have been able to move ahead. I think by doing so, I finally became the man I should have always been: kind, humble, and grateful."

Almost everyone experiences negative self-talk, and just about everyone is scared. It's OK. The eureka moment:

Self-talk, and the anxiety that comes with it, is an unspoken normal. We all have it. We all live with it. We're here to help you overcome the fear and move past the doubt.

The Battle of Self-Talk

We seriously considered calling this book *The Battle of Self-Talk*. Another idea was *The Battle of You*, because you are literally not alone in that mind of yours. Life is an inner battle of You vs. You. As much as you may wish your determined Maverick—willpower and all—were sitting in the catbird seat 24/7, that's simply not the case.

You don't get to vote your Monster off your island, but you do get a say in how you choose to crack it open. In the chapters that follow in Part One, let's put in the work to better understand what sends your personal Monster into a tizzy. Remember, the Monster is as ordinary as the air you breathe. It's your personalized version of "batteries included" that comes in every human set. So, we need to figure out ways to live with this unwanted roommate who scoffs when you tell them to leave.

This is a journey of self-discovery which leads invariably to one of the most powerful life skills of all: self-leadership.

Before that skill can be mastered, we need to take a closer look at some of the more prevalent cognitive saboteurs that might feed your beast. Having an awareness of where the Monster voice comes from and how it likes to operate is key to understanding how it slows you down.

We've now set the stage for Part One. As you turn the page to discover what your Monster might feast on, it's mission critical to take into the next chapters the following three truths:

1. Your inner narratives are largely made up of other people's stated opinions of you. Ironically, these narratives often have very little to do with you. They reflect the other person's own self-doubts.
2. You're cloudy on what's actually true about you.
3. You have to create your own inner story after decades of accepting the mosaic from everyone else.

Have you already experienced this moment? You're way ahead!

So what fuels your Monster?

The rest of Part One breaks down six self-talk saboteurs that most often nourish your inner beast—starting with impostor syndrome and ending with overthinking.

We're all constantly in the process of learning and growing. No one ever truly arrives or is finished with this process. The idea is to learn to talk to ourselves in a way that makes us more energized and more determined, not to derail ourselves by ruminating on self-defeating prophesies each day. Go easy on yourself and try to enjoy the ride. You'll come out the other side with more clarity, more confidence, more tools, more time, more ammunition for dealing with the Pauls of the world and, above all, more productivity.

2

Impostor Syndrome

Successful people have fears, successful people have doubts, and successful people have worries. They just don't let these feelings stop them.

T. HARV EKER

IF YOU added up the combined fingers of the three authors, you still wouldn't have enough to count the number of books visionary author, thought leader, and keynote speaker Seth Godin has filled. From *Purple Cow* to *This Is Strategy*, Seth has made a living uncracking the insightful, nuanced things that make humans who they are. A few years back, Seth was the headlining keynote speaker at the 2017 Digital Summit in Denver, where he unleashed a "Godinism" to make sense of the condition known as impostor syndrome.

You've probably heard the term *impostor syndrome*. It refers to the feeling of self-doubt, anxiety, or inadequacy despite evidence of competence. It means you feel like a fraud, even though you've done the hard work to be where you are. This term originated in a 1978 paper by psychologists Suzanne Imes and Pauline Rose Clance on their study of successful businesswomen, but it resonates with everyone.

Godin's take on it is simple: when you hear that little voice inside your head saying you are not qualified, it's just a data point. The little voice chirping "not qualified" is the Monster. The other voice, the one that reminds you of your potential, is your Maverick.

Jonathan Forstot is an experienced marketing executive with a diverse portfolio across various industries. A former director of brand marketing at Taylor Guitars, he told us how impostor syndrome played out for him at a brand he was leading after his rock star days. He said, "A couple years into building the brand and marketing department, the CEO asked me, 'Do we even need marketing?' You can imagine the inner dialogue that set off: *Have I accomplished anything? Is this guy clueless? Have I done enough to educate him about the value of marketing? Am I a shitty marketer? Am I a fraud?*"

Jonathan is in no way a fraud. He's built brand strategies for some of the best-known companies in the world. His approach is wholly unique, and yet, a casual (and careless) inquiry from a fellow executive sent his mind to the metaphorical mosh pit.

Welcome to the Club

You might have experienced the feeling that you're not as good as your achievements suggest. But you may not realize how many other people mistrust their abilities, regardless of their remarkable successes. According to a study published in 2011 in the *International Journal of Behavioral Science*, an estimated 70 percent of people experience impostor syndrome at some point in their lives. It's most prevalent among high-achieving individuals, especially women and minorities. The International Coaching Federation released another study saying 85 percent of coaches have encountered clients with impostor syndrome, revealing it's extremely common in professional settings.

In short, the Monster rules the minds of over 235 million Americans. Sadly, most people haven't learned how to take command of their Monsters by relying on their energy, positivity, and helpful internal messages, and this is especially true in stressful situations. In a room of one hundred people, just thirty of them have mastered their mental narratives. Imagine being asked to stand up if you are among the remaining seventy people. You have a lot of company in the fight against yourself, and your decision-making is seriously compromised when you're paralyzed with fear.

Many highly accomplished people have spoken openly about their self-doubt and fear of being exposed as frauds despite evidence to the contrary. Here are a few examples:

- Nobel Prize–winning physicist Albert Einstein reportedly suffered from feelings of ineptitude and even described himself as an "involuntary swindler," despite his enormous contributions to science.

- The legendary actress Meryl Streep has said she struggles with feelings of incompetence and is "waiting for the other shoe to drop" when it comes to her success.

- Poet and author Maya Angelou once said, "Each time I write a book, every time I face that yellow pad, the challenge is so great. I have written eleven books, but each time I think, 'Uh oh, they're going to find out now. I've run a game on everybody, and they're going to find me out.'"

- Actor Tom Hanks has spoken freely about his struggles with self-doubt even after winning two Oscars, seven Emmys, and four Golden Globes. In a 2016 interview with NPR, he said, "No matter what we've done, there comes a point where you think, 'How did I get here? When are they going to discover that I am, in fact, a fraud and take everything away from me?'"

- Former COO of Facebook Sheryl Sandberg acknowledged in her book *Lean In*, "Every time I was called on in class, I was sure that I was about to embarrass myself. Every time I took a test, I was sure that it had gone badly. And every time I didn't embarrass myself—or even excelled—I believed that I had fooled everyone yet again. One day soon, the jig would be up."

- In an interview with *The New York Times*, former CEO of Starbucks Howard Schultz admitted to feeling undeserving and insecure. He said, "Very few people, whether you've been in that job before or not, get into the seat and believe today that they are now qualified to be the CEO. They're not going to tell you that, but it's true."

- Sonia Sotomayor, the first Hispanic Supreme Court justice, also admitted to feeling like a fraud. As she once said in a speech, "I have spent my years since Princeton... not feeling completely a part of the worlds I inhabit. I am always looking over my shoulder, wondering if I measure up."

And these are just a few examples. We could write an entire book about people who admit their Monsters are in charge more often than they'd like.

As you can see, even people commonly regarded as the most accomplished in their fields experience extreme self-doubt, and it's often accompanied by feelings of loneliness. For people who suffer from impostor syndrome, success is a constant battle because any praise they earn doesn't make sense to them. They feel like they're bluffing their way through life, and the constant fear of exposure haunts them. With each success, they think, "I was lucky. I fooled everyone this time, but will my luck hold when people discover that I'm not up to the job?"

Our guess is you've read this far because you've found yourself falling into the 70 percent of people just like this. In America, that makes you part of a colossal unspoken party. Welcome to the 235M Impostor Syndrome Club! If the number holds globally, it would be "The 6B Club." So, while you may feel alone, you're far from being the only one navigating Monster Island.

What if the Determined You could flip the script on impostor syndrome? Could you wrap your head around the concept that feeling like a fraud is actually a sign of growth?

Or, as Godin suggests, accept that feeling like an impostor is nothing more than a data point, an indicator that you're nudging yourself outside of your comfort zone.

> **MAVERICK PRO TIP**
>
> When you embark on something new, important, or challenging, it's quite normal to feel abnormal about your abilities. In other words, telling yourself, "Hey, I'm not a fraud. I'm just stretching and growing my courage muscles right now," is the determined Maverick part of your mind sparring with your Monster.

Headamentals: Self-Awareness Assessment

This brief assessment will help you understand the extent to which you tend to suffer from impostor syndrome. It's a short list of statements that describe specific thought patterns. Please consider the extent to which you agree or disagree with each statement and assign each response the appropriate numerical value:

Strongly Disgree: 1
Disagree: 2
Neither Agree nor Disagree: 3
Agree: 4
Strongly Agree: 5

Set aside ten minutes to complete this assessment in a quiet place. For the most accurate results, choose the first answer that comes to mind—and be honest.

1. When I compare myself to others, I don't measure up. _____

2. I'm more likely to dwell on my mistakes than my successes. _____

3. I set unrealistically high standards for myself and feel disappointed when I don't meet them. _____

4. I feel uncomfortable showcasing my talents and accomplishments. _____

5. I attribute my successes more to luck than to my abilities or hard work. _____

6. I feel like I don't deserve my success. _____

7. I doubt my abilities even when I've demonstrated competence in a particular area. _____

8. I downplay my accomplishments when I'm talking to people. _____

9. It's hard for me to relax because I feel guilty if I'm not constantly pushing myself. _____

10. I find it difficult to accept recognition or positive feedback about my work. _____

11. I worry that people will discover I'm not as skilled or knowledgeable as they think I am. _____

12. I'm hesitant to take credit for my achievements. _____

13. I'm surprised when I achieve a positive outcome, even when I've worked hard. _____

14. I tend to overprepare for things because I don't think my regular effort will be sufficient. _____

15. When someone gives me constructive feedback, I tend to focus more on the opportunities for improvement rather than the things I'm doing well. _____

16. My fear of failure leads me to work longer hours than necessary. _____

TOTAL _____

Add up your points to determine your impostor syndrome tendencies. The total score will range from 16 to 80.

16–32 points: Minimal impostor syndrome tendencies. You have a confident, well-grounded sense of who you are and feel secure in your abilities. Even when you have a fleeting moment of self-doubt, you quickly recognize that it's a normal part of being human. You appreciate genuine praise and see constructive feedback as useful input. In short, you maintain a healthy balance—acknowledging areas for growth while firmly believing in your own value and abilities.

33–56 points: Moderate impostor syndrome tendencies. You usually trust your skills, but every now and then, a nagging doubt creeps in. You know you've achieved a lot, yet sometimes you wonder if you truly deserve all the praise you get. You might brush off compliments, attributing your success to luck or timing rather than your abilities. When feedback comes your way, you appreciate it, but it can also trigger that inner critic, making you question your competence. It's a constant balancing act between acknowledging your hard work and wrestling with the occasional fear that you might be "faking it" in some way.

More than 56 points: Strong impostor syndrome tendencies. You probably often feel like you're not quite good enough, no matter how much you've achieved. Even though others see your accomplishments, you struggle to fully accept them as your own. You constantly worry that one day someone will realize you're not as capable as they think and that your success is just a fluke. Compliments feel uncomfortable, and you tend to brush them off, convinced that you don't truly deserve them. Feedback can feel overwhelming, igniting doubts about your abilities and making you question if you're truly cut out for your role. There's a constant fear that you're only pretending to know what you're doing, and eventually, everyone will find out.

How did you do? If you're like most people, you probably didn't fall in the 16–32 point range. Congratulations: you're human!

Strategies to Overcome Self-Doubt

Tom Braun wasn't always president of the LA Galaxy, a club with legendary lore, including winning more Major League Soccer championships than any other club in the history of the league. For almost a decade, Tom worked his way up the ranks. Despite the Galaxy's many impressive acclaims, it had been a long time since Landon Donovan, David Beckham, or any other all-star Galaxy player had hoisted one of those trophies. When the AEG lost their patience and decided to shuffle things up at the top, they tapped Tom to be the new president of business operations and COO.

Tom has worked closely with Ryan on his transition from operations lead to leadership lead. The two shared plenty of walks and talks to squelch some of the self-doubt that was weighing on Tom's mind. Was he ready? He knew he was strong on the numbers side, but could he lead people?

One of the first presidential decisions Tom made was to hire Ryan's company, Courageous, to lead the Galaxy's first ever full staff offsite. While Tom still wrestled with self-doubt, they designed an agenda to show Tom's human side. They also came up with a vision for the club: *Fight for the Fan.*

Much was accomplished at that offsite, and real conversations were had. Tom gave the staff permission to speak bluntly and freely. The team openly discussed how Galaxy lost LA-fan support to their neighbor and rival, LAFC. Tom did not shy away from the problem. His confidence grew while his self-doubt shrank. The offsite brought the team closer together, and when the season was upon them, they were ready to "fight for the fan."

Nine months after Tom accepted the job, and in his first full year leading the business, the LA Galaxy found themselves back on the podium. For the first time in a decade, they won Major League Soccer's most coveted trophy. They were champions once again.

The struggle with self-doubt is particularly tricky for leaders because individual self-doubt often transforms into team-doubt. And when you lose the team, it's hard to win them back. Rather than beating yourself up, let's talk about strategies to overcome moments, days, or even weeks of self-doubt.

As a first step, acknowledge that feelings of self-doubt are common. Even people who appear to be self-assured and highly successful grapple in private moments with a lack of confidence. Accepting that this is normal helps reduce the stigma and isolation associated with impostor syndrome. If you start to criticize yourself for feeling less than or to doubt yourself, recall the Nobel Prize winners, Supreme Court justices, acclaimed business leaders, and award-winning actors who share those thoughts. You're in good company.

Something you'll hear us say again and again: reflect on your achievements. When you recall past successes, you're reminded of what you are capable of. One of Suzy's colleagues, Joyel Crawford, is an award-winning career coach, writer, and speaker. She created a "DIG" folder, which stands for "Damn, I'm Good!" Whenever Joyel gets a complimentary email or text about a presentation she gave or a meeting she facilitated, she drops it in her DIG folder. When things don't go as well as she expected or she doubts herself, she flips through the folder as a reminder of how talented and impactful she is.

Even people who appear to be self-assured and highly successful grapple with a lack of confidence.

A DIG folder like Joyel's is easy to create, and once you get into the habit of dropping praise for your work into it, you'll appreciate having quick access to those reminders.

> **MAVERICK PRO TIP**
>
> When your Maverick tells you that you're doing something well, pay attention. Write yourself a note and drop it in your DIG folder. Always be on the lookout for messages that build you up. And when you find yourself thinking you're an incapable louse, cast that idea aside ASAP. Don't let it take root. Don't be afraid to build your arsenal of "humble brag" confidence points. Save the emails, texts, and notes people send to compliment your work. You can turn to this folder from time to time to defuse self-doubt and restore your confidence.

List at least three achievements to remind yourself that you can accomplish great things.

_____

_____

_____

Another essential strategy to combat impostor syndrome is to set realistic expectations. Instead of striving for perfection, focus on doing your best and learning from your experiences. This shift in mindset allows you to see challenges as opportunities to learn and grow.

It also helps to seek guidance from people you trust as you're coming up the learning curve. External validation provides a stable foundation when it feels like the earth is moving under your feet.

Let's face it. In many ways, we are all living solitary lives. According to data from the US Bureau of Labor Statistics (2020), when calculating the amount of time people spend alone during the day, the average adult aged fifteen and older, living solo, spent 11.3 waking hours by themselves. Add in a good night's sleep, and someone who lives with only their Monster and Maverick is looking at over nineteen hours of isolation in a day. That equals 80 percent of their lives stuck inside their heads!

The same study suggested that those living with a roommate or a partner experience seven hours of time in solitude, or fifteen out of twenty-four hours when you add in sleep time. Layer on the lasting effects of the pandemic, hybrid work, and the ability to DoorDash or Amazon your way into never leaving your pajamas, and you can see how we have an isolation epidemic on our hands (and in our heads).

This is why you need to work extra hard to find people to talk to, rely on, learn from, and trust; people who will give it to you straight because they care.

While it may feel like it takes an eternity to build real relationships with colleagues at work, you need friends who can help you climb the ladder, not in isolation, but together. Be less like the woodpecker—birds notorious for living solitary lives—and more like the crab—distinguished for scuttling sideways across the sand. Walk sideways. Make friends. Go together.

So, where to start?

You know that colleague who isn't shy about pointing out the poppy seed that's stuck in your teeth? Bingo. That's the person you need by your side. Find people who aren't afraid to speak the truth and who can deliver tough love from time to time without being a jerk about it. And don't forget it's a two-way street. Which peers will you show up for, even when it's hard?

Headamentals: Set Realistic Expectations and Find Your Friends

Using the prompts below, name at least two unrealistic expectations you've set for yourself. Next, create a more accurate expectation and identify who you can reach out to for input and guidance.

Unrealistic Expectation 1:

_____

_____

More accurate expectation:

_____

_____

Colleagues I can call on to give it to me straight:

_____

_____

Unrealistic Expectation 2:

_____

_____

More accurate expectation:

_____

_____

Colleagues I can call on to give it to me straight:

_____

_____

Overcoming impostor syndrome is an ongoing challenge. It requires spotting negative thoughts as soon as they surface and immediately replacing them with positive, affirming messages. Doing so is not only possible, but also being aware of impostor-type thoughts is a sign that you are stretching and growing. And while you may never be able to declare total victory, the more you can identify and combat self-doubt, the more you'll be able to fully celebrate your talents, potential, and accomplishments.

Self-Handicapping

Doubt kills more dreams than failure ever will.

SUZY KASSEM

IT'S HARD to imagine that the LEGO Group was ever on the brink of bankruptcy. In 2004, many of the toy company's employees believed the root cause was external, like the rise in popularity of video games. However, new CEO Jørgen Vig Knudstorp spotted a different source: the company's very own people.

Knudstorp acknowledged that many of LEGO Group's problems stemmed from internal inefficiencies, in particular cumbersome decision-making processes and mismanagement at a variety of levels. Was the slowdown self-inflicted because the team was afraid of what was to come from the video game industry? Or was it a focus problem?

Knudstorp surmised that no one was getting in the way of the brand's success but LEGO itself. The organization's internal culture was self-sabotaging. He tackled the issue head-on by re-centering the company on its core strength—the brick-building business—and launched a turnaround initiative that would propel LEGO to new heights of success. His ability to recognize and admit to internal sabotage saved the company, and it's a cautionary tale about how leaders can accidentally cripple their own organizations.

Until you're able to consistently replace the fear of inadequacy with the assurance that you are fine just the way you are, you may find yourself falling into the quicksand known as self-handicapping. Self-handicapping is the practice of deliberately creating obstacles to avoid taking responsibility for less-than-stellar outcomes and the pain of negative feedback.

It's a classic Monster move, first theorized in 1978 by psychologists Steven Berglas and Edward E. Jones. Their concept of self-handicapping focuses on the strategies and mechanisms people use to protect their self-esteem and self-worth in situations where failure is possible.

Here are a few stories of people who demonstrate the subliminal art of self-handicapping. Perhaps you can relate to one or more of them.

Chris was recently promoted to VP of marketing. She was the newest member of the executive team of an $18 billion division of a global powerhouse. It was a significant promotion, and she wasn't sure she'd be able to hold her own. She was scheduled to fly out with the team on Sunday night for a five-day performance review of the European business units. That morning, Chris decided to eat a three-day-old chocolate éclair she'd been saving for just the right moment. As she wolfed it down, she wondered, fleetingly, if the custard had spoiled. Several hours later, when she crawled from the bathroom to tell her boss she was suffering from food poisoning, she wondered if she were secretly afraid of not being ready for her debut on the international stage.

Jack was his company's star sales rep until his boss poached the top earner from their toughest competitor. Since then, Jack hasn't been sure of his place in the organization. Luckily, after months of relentless effort, his biggest prospect was finally ready to talk about a deal. As the enormity of the opportunity became the talk of the office, Jack's excitement was mixed with anxiety. Instead of immersing himself in crafting a winning proposal that identified the prospect's needs and his company's unique solutions, he busied himself with distractions. He scheduled unnecessary meetings with longtime clients, talked endlessly with his colleagues, and spent extra time at the gym. The night before the big meeting, Jack scrambled to complete the presentation, his heart racing with each keystroke. Exhausted, he stepped back to review it, but deep down he knew he hadn't given it his all.

Tom had been bucking for a promotion for a year. As the months flew by and he didn't get the nod, he grew more and more discouraged. Faced with a looming deadline for a crucial project, he found himself falling behind. Instead of acknowledging his shortcomings and seeking help, he casually mentioned to his coworkers that he'd been feeling under the weather for days, hoping they'd understand if the quality of his work suffered. During team meetings, he frequently emphasized how demanding the project was, subtly preparing the team for his potential failure. He also made vague references to personal issues, suggesting that they too might impact his performance. On the day of the project presentation, Tom appeared disheveled and unprepared. He knew he was sabotaging his own success, but in his mind, it was better to blame external factors than face the embarrassment of not meeting the team's expectations.

The Self-Handicapping Habit

As these stories demonstrate, self-handicapping involves setting yourself up for failure before an event even occurs. By making it more difficult to succeed, you have a built-in excuse for anything less than an exceptional outcome, and you protect your self-esteem in the process.

As we saw in the previous scenarios, commonly used self-handicapping tactics include the following:

- Delaying a project until the last minute to justify why your work isn't up to par.
- Paralysis from having too many things on your plate and not letting anyone know until it's too late. Or, not having the courage to clarify which priority is the most important.
- Failing to adequately prepare for a task or event, giving you an excuse if you don't perform as well as you expected.
- Showing up to an important event exhausted or distracted, providing a built-in reason for failure.
- Abusing drugs or alcohol so you can attribute your poor performance to being under the influence, thus avoiding responsibility for the outcome.

Self-handicappers rely on these behaviors to avoid taking responsibility for their failures without even realizing it. If you find yourself relating to any of these methods, hit the brakes. It means you're sabotaging yourself at work, in your personal life, or both. If these behaviors go unchecked, they will prevent you from achieving your goals and reaching your full potential.

The good news is there are actions you can take to get yourself back on track. We've outlined a couple of suggestions here. Though they look like the strategies for dealing with impostor syndrome, there are some important nuances:

Self-awareness: The first step is to recognize and acknowledge that you engage in self-handicapping behaviors.

Recognize the cost: The next step is to understand the negative consequences of self-handicapping. While creating built-in explanations for poor performance may protect your self-esteem temporarily, in the long run it impacts your ability to live up to your potential and can damage your reputation and your relationships.

> **MAVERICK PRO TIP**
>
> Turn to that colleague who'd call out the poppy seeds in your teeth and ask if they see you exhibiting self-handicapping tendencies. Don't have that friend yet? Go to our website (headamentals.com/mavericks) to join our private Headamentals group. We'll pair you with an accountability partner who will set you straight.

Headamentals: Identify Self-Imposed Barriers

Take a few minutes to reflect on your behavior patterns and identify instances where you have used excuses or created barriers to avoid giving your best effort on something important.

Situation 1

I engaged in self-handicapping behavior by:

_____

_____

_____

The price I paid for self-handicapping in this instance was:

_____

_____

_____

Situation 2
Another time I engaged in self-handicapping behavior by:

___

___

___

The price I paid for self-handicapping in this instance was:

___

___

___

Situation 3
Another time I engaged in self-handicapping behavior by:

___

___

___

The price I paid for self-handicapping in this instance was:

___

___

___

Reframe How You Think About Challenges

Chip Conley is a modern elder and master in wisdom. Like most folks who exude next-level intelligence, that's not the way Chip would describe himself. He has lived a business-launching adventure that includes founding Joie de Vivre

Accept that failure is a natural part of the learning process.

Hospitality, one of the largest boutique hotel brands in America. He then became head of global hospitality and strategy at Airbnb, where he worked directly with the founders to transform the company into the multinational brand it is today. If you're looking for a little wisdom, you can find it in any one of Chip's books, including *Wisdom at Work: The Making of a Modern Elder*. Or you can see him for yourself at his Modern Elder Academy, a midlife wisdom school that helps individuals navigate transitions in life and career, in either of two locations: Baja, Mexico, and Santa Fe, New Mexico.

Chip is living a courageous life and footing the bill to make his dream an operationalized reality. Investing in your own wellness destination can get expensive, and fast! One of the mechanisms Chip uses to lower the stakes in his brain, or to toot his own horn when he gets a win, he says, is to "literally say out loud, 'Yay, Chipper!' as if my dad is coaching me in Little League baseball. I probably say this, on average, once a day, and it feels good to have that self-affirmation." In this way, Chip has figured out a way to reframe the challenge in front of him.

Rather than seeing unfamiliar or difficult tasks as threatening, think of them as opportunities to stop self-handicapping. Acknowledge that by continually stretching and taking on new assignments, you're expanding your knowledge, building your capacity, and enlarging your circle of influence. As a side benefit, you'll build self-confidence, and, over time, you'll be more likely to take on complex assignments without stashing land mines in the shrubbery.

Accept that failure is a natural part of the learning process. Analyze the situations where you didn't measure up to understand what went wrong and how you can improve next time.

Finally, find someone who will hold you accountable. Share what you've learned about self-handicapping with someone you trust: a colleague, a friend, or a mentor. And be sure to let them know every time you make the courageous decision to take on a demanding new project. Ask them to give you feedback on your progress and cheer you on when the going gets tough. This kind of support helps you stay aware of the tendency to self-handicap and reduces the urge to do so.

Headamentals: Accountability Reframe

Spend a few minutes reflecting on the three examples of self-handicapping you unearthed in the previous exercise. Much like the Headamentals training in the previous chapter on impostor syndrome, think about how you could have reframed the challenge so it didn't seem so daunting and who you could have asked to hold you accountable.

Self-Handicapping Situation 1
(from the previous exercise)

Possible reframe:
_____

_____

_____

Colleague I can ask to hold me accountable:
_____

_____

Self-Handicapping Situation 2
(from the previous exercise)

Possible reframe: _____
_____
_____

Colleague I can ask to hold me accountable: _____
_____

Self-Handicapping Situation 3
(from the previous exercise)

Possible reframe: _____
_____
_____

Colleague I can ask to hold me accountable: _____
_____

Headamentals: Write a Letter to Your Monster

Before we move on, it's time to write a note to your Monster so you can get to know it better.

Here's a powerful letter that one of Suzy's executive friends wrote to her Monster so you can get a sense of what such a missive looks like.

My Monster's Name: Work Harder
I have worked so much in my short forty-one years.
I have worked to the point of exhaustion.
I have worked through three pregnancies until the moment of giving birth.
I have worked at the expense of every other aspect of my life.
I worked until it made me sick.
You know what, Work Harder? I am done.
I will not Work Harder just because I have been conditioned to do so.
You are a myth—a lie.
Your lie is that you are the key to success.
Your lie is that you are the cornerstone of my value.
But I now know that my value, skills, capability, and success are not solely reliant on you.
I am done martyring myself to you.
I will not Work Harder even if I like the work.
I will not Work Harder even if there is a higher purpose.
I will work, but not on your terms.
I will work on my terms and in harmony with the rest of my life.

NABEELA ELSAYED, *former Executive Vice President and Chief Operations Officer, Walmart Canada*

By taking the time to directly address her Work Harder Monster, Nabeela gave breath to her empowering Maverick. Now, it's your turn.

What are your Monster's most powerful qualities?

_____

_____

What is the source of its power?

_____

_____

How might you literally address your Monster?

_____

_____

What would you like to say to it?

_____

_____

Write a note to your Monster and tell it how you feel about it.

_____

_____

_____

_____

Why are we asking you to partake in this exercise? As famous ring king Mike Tyson once shared, "Everyone has a plan until they get punched in the mouth." Writing a note to your Monster helps you to better prepare for those unexpected inner conversations when they show themselves and to stop self-handicapping before it gets out of hand.

We also hope you'll have the courage to share the letter you wrote to your Monster in our private Headamentals group (headamentals.com/mavericks). Then, peruse the feed and read other letters from those who are part of our Headamentals community.

Confirmation Bias

> Your mind is your best friend. But it can also be your worst enemy.
>
> **SHIRZAD CHAMINE**

IN THE SPIRIT of keeping with classic movies that date the authors, have you ever stumbled into the 2008 comedy *Step Brothers*? There's an unforgettable moment when the hilarious tandem of Will Ferrell and John C. Reilly's characters, two grown men forced to live together as stepbrothers, have a much-needed breakthrough. Initially at odds, their rivalry reaches a boiling point until they discover they have more in common than they thought and bond over their shared love for quirky things like "karate in the garage" and their favorite movies. In that split second of realization, they look at each other and say, "Did we just become best friends?"

While we believe that it's important to make friends at work, you also need to be cautious to avoid thinking like everyone else in your company. Avoiding "groupthink" reminds us of a certain CEO who goes out of his way to hire people who think differently or secures, as we like to call it, confirmation bias insurance.

Reed Hastings, cofounder and co-CEO of Netflix, has built a corporate culture that's all about innovation, freedom, and responsibility. What makes this culture thrive is his belief in the power of diverse perspectives. From the start, Hastings knew that it would hold Netflix back if he surrounded himself with people who thought and acted just like he did. So, he made it a priority to hire individuals with different backgrounds, experiences, and approaches—people who weren't afraid to challenge his thinking.

Netflix's incredible growth trajectory—from a DVD rental company to a global streaming giant—owes much to this strategy. Hastings actively encouraged open debate and constructive conflict, convinced that a variety of viewpoints leads to better decisions and helps the company stay agile in a fast-changing world. By avoiding the common mistake of hiring "clones," he created a culture where innovation could truly flourish.

His approach, detailed in Netflix's culture deck and in his book, *No Rules Rules: Netflix and the Culture of Reinvention*, serves as a reminder for leaders: embracing different perspectives is key to building a forward-thinking, dynamic organization. It's also a surefire way to avoid confirmation bias.

Confirmation bias is the all-too-human cognitive phenomenon of seeking out, interpreting, and remembering information in a way that confirms your existing beliefs and ignoring or dismissing contradictory evidence.

Social psychologist Leon Festinger says that when confronted with new information, people have an inherent tendency to ensure it is consistent with what they already believe to be true.

Think about how passionately a sports fan will defend "their" team even when they're at the bottom of the league table. When their team loses a game, die-hard supporters often attribute the lopsided score to a bad ref or an off day, and they tend to surround themselves with others who share their views. This enables them to avoid the tension of having to rethink what they've believed to be true in the past.

At its core, confirmation bias is a way for our brains to conserve mental energy. When we encounter information that's consistent with what we believe, our brains relax in the comfort of familiar ideas, which triggers positive emotions. In contrast, when faced with things that challenge what we "know" to be true, our brains become stressed.

Our goal is to help you make confirmation bias work for you, not against you.

Headamentals: Are Your Beliefs Working for You, or Against You?

Take a few minutes to reflect on situations where confirmation bias worked for you and against you.

Here's a situation where confirmation bias was a force for good in my life:

_____

_____

_____

Here's a situation where confirmation bias fueled the Monster in my mind:

_____

_____

_____

Here's another situation where confirmation bias was a force for good in my life:

_____

_____

_____

Here's another situation where confirmation bias fueled the Monster in my mind:

_____

_____

_____

Seeking validation for your beliefs by surrounding yourself with others who agree with you is a common human tendency. Though finding commonality can be a bonding experience, as it was for the stepbrothers, it can also keep us anchored in stale approaches or outdated thinking. Awareness of confirmation bias and how it can limit us, and our organizations, is a powerful self-awareness tool, as it was for Netflix.

Experiential Avoidance

I'm convinced that about half of what separates successful entrepreneurs from non-successful ones is pure perseverance… You have to show up, even when you don't want to.

STEVE JOBS

PICTURE THIS: Actually... don't. A not-so-great-moment in business history came (and went) when Kodak failed to embrace digital photography, even though they had invented it. Despite masterminding the first digital camera in 1975, Kodak's leadership resisted moving forward with digital photography because they feared it would cannibalize their highly profitable film business. And in many ways, they feared right!

Experiential avoidance occurs when you are faced with something you perceive as uncomfortable or threatening. By avoiding it, you escape anything that might come with it: failure, awkwardness, embarrassment, or even physical harm. When you avoid the "thing" that seems dangerous, you suffer the illusion that you feel better. You don't have to fail or feel bad, or worse, reinforce the story that you are, in fact, not good enough.

However, experiential avoidance has been shown to intensify psychological stress and have long-term negative consequences such as increased anxiety, depression, and other mental health issues. When you avoid something, you never learn the skills necessary to deal with fear, tension, or even small discomforts. You actively weaken yourself by choosing to listen to the mental alarm bells that tell you to run away, but your actions are based on sheer speculation. Your projections are fully fabricated, fully fictitious, and fully full of it. And that person or event you're avoiding? They're still there, waiting to be dealt with when you pull your head out of the sand.

Here are some examples of experiential avoidance we've witnessed in the people we coach.

Sara was tagged as "high potential" early in her career. As a result, she was given opportunities to talk about her research in front of the senior leaders and high-value clients of the organization she worked for. Despite being well prepared, she misjudged the audience in a recent presentation, and her comments missed the mark. As someone who was accustomed to receiving rave reviews, Sara started to doubt herself as a professional and an individual. Ever since that presentation, she's been "too busy" to accept new opportunities to showcase her work.

John is a first-generation IT specialist who grew up in Haiti and immigrated to the United States when he was a teenager. He has been successful at work and has lots of friends. But he struggles romantically. He thought his relationship with Emily would last forever. He dreamed of the house they'd buy, the children they'd have, and the joy they'd share for many years to come. When Emily broke up with him seemingly out of the blue, he decided to get a dog rather than risk another heartbreak.

Abby has always had a testy relationship with Ralph. In fact, just passing him in the hall makes her nervous. She finds him arrogant and tells her work friends he has a Napoleon complex. In a recent meeting, Ralph made a snide remark about her analysis of the company's proposed profit-sharing payout. Since then, she's made a point of having a prior commitment whenever they're scheduled to be in the same gathering.

Headamentals: Get to the Other Side of Doubt

Take a few minutes to reflect on instances in your recent past when you've practiced experiential avoidance.

Situation 1
An example of coming face-to-face with something or someone that made me doubt myself is:

_____

_____

_____

Here's how I avoided it:

_____

_____

_____

Here's the price I'm paying for avoiding this situation:

_____

_____

_____

Situation 2
Another example of coming face-to-face with something or someone that made me doubt myself is:

_____

_____

_____

Here's how I avoided it:

_____

_____

_____

Here's the price I'm paying for avoiding this situation:

_____

_____

_____

Situation 3

A third example of coming face-to-face with something or someone that made me doubt myself is:

_____

_____

_____

Here's how I avoided it:

_____

_____

_____

Here's the price I'm paying for avoiding this situation:

_____

_____

_____

Now, take a deep breath, and repeat after us: It's not your fault. Let it go.

To be fair, most of us have never learned to operate beyond our standard Monster mentality. We often don't even realize we're operating under the Monster's spell, but now you know. The trains of life have us arriving early or late on the "real us" for all sorts of reasons. As Bill Burnett, coauthor of *Designing Your Life*, said in a TEDx Talk, "Start from where you are. You're not late for anything." If you can get yourself to a healthy mindset and stop avoiding uncomfortable run-ins or experiences, it'll be a train ride worth taking.

The Amygdala Hijack

What one does
is what counts and
not what one
had the intention
of doing.

PABLO PICASSO

It's hard to believe it's been over twenty years since *8 Mile* premiered on the big screen. The film stars Marshall Bruce Mathers III, aka Eminem, and is loosely based on his own life. Early in the film, his character, Jimmy "B-Rabbit" Smith Jr., a young rapper from Detroit, desperately wants to compete in a rap battle and escape the hardships of growing up poor in a run-down trailer park. Paralyzed by the fear of performing onstage, he tries to summon courage during a bathroom pre-show pep talk. The audience feels connected to B-Rabbit. They can relate to his struggle, and they're rooting for the young rapper from the edge of their seats. It's gut-wrenching to watch B-Rabbit choke onstage when his self-doubt gets the best of him. He is unable to perform.

Luckily for the world, Eminem found a way to overcome his fears in real life. Mathers has openly discussed his struggles with stage fright and emphasizes the importance of preparation and practice. The more prepared he was, the quieter his Monster became and the more he was able to lean in to his Maverick self.

The amygdala is a small almond-shaped cluster of nuclei in the brain. It is responsible for processing feelings and memories and plays a crucial role in managing and regulating emotions. It can easily overwhelm the normal decision-making that occurs in your prefrontal cortex and override your ability to think rationally and make considered judgments.

An "amygdala hijack" occurs when the brain operates in a heightened stress response. Daniel Goleman coined the phrase in his book *Emotional Intelligence*, where he describes what happens when someone perceives a threat or experiences strong emotions like fear, anger, and anxiety. Your brain is literally taken over by the familiar "fight, flight, or freeze" response, which can lead to behavior that is out of character or inappropriate for the situation, often displayed through impulsive or irrational actions you later regret. When your brain detects a threat, it directs oxygenated blood away from your prefrontal cortex, where decisions are made, and toward the areas in your body that can physically respond to the threat. If left unchecked, it leads to a slew of consequences, including prolonged stress and operating from a position of scarcity rather than abundance.

Imagine a team meeting in which Adrienne has just finished presenting her work on an important project. Immediately, one of her colleagues questions her approach and another voices his concern. Instead of calmly restating her rationale, Adrienne's heart begins racing and her stomach is in a knot. She snaps defensively, escalating the situation unnecessarily. Sound familiar?

Hijacking the Hijack

In their book, *Playing the Long Game: A Handbook for Parenting Elite and College Athletes*, Maureen Breeze and Dr. Suzanne Schimmel recommend slow-paced belly breathing as one of the most effective ways to counter a stress-inducing incident. "It puts the brakes on a triggering emotion and sends an 'all safe' signal to the mind and body. Even focusing on a single breath, focusing on a deliberate and slow exhale, can begin to turn down the volume on intense feelings."

Imagine what this slow-paced belly breathing signals to your Monster: *Hey, Monster. It's going to be OK, you big Donkey Kong. I appreciate you signaling a threat, but let's take a moment to calm down.*

Breeze and Schimmel also observe that when you're hungry, angry, lonely, or tired (what they refer to in their book as HALT), you're likely to fall prey to impulses and emotional reactions that interfere with your goals. While your Monster is hell-bent on knocking you off track, your Maverick understands that success and happiness require a balance. Your Maverick will take everything into consideration—the good, the bad, and the ugly—before deciding.

Buddhists call this a state of "non-attachment." Your Maverick hears and appreciates the information that can hold you back (for example, when you ask yourself, "what if I fail?"), but like a badass brain ninja, your Maverick is able to push through. It centers on the best, most true, and most useful information without becoming attached to the outcome.

When fear of failure is front and center, people are inclined to warp the truth or converge on self-limiting details. It's confirmation bias in action. Asking yourself "What's the worst thing that can happen?" is freeing if you're able to answer the question honestly. Nine times out of ten, the worst-case scenario isn't all that bad. It's like imagining there's a dragon under your bed, but realizing it's only a dust bunny when you get down on the floor to check it out. And even if there really is a dragon lying in wait, you have more resilience and strength than you give yourself credit for.

Your Maverick acknowledges the mental junk food the Monster consumes but also asks nonjudgmental, meaningful, clarifying questions to get a more accurate sense of what is true. This enables you to make calculated decisions from a calm, alert state instead of an anxious, fearful, emotional state.

When you allow your Maverick to take over, your brain flips the conversation on its head by staying open. It doesn't just ask "What's the worst thing that can happen?" Michelle Poler, the author of *Hello, Fears: Crush Your Comfort Zone and Become Who You're Meant to Be*, advises us to fully flip the script by asking ourselves, "What's *the best thing* that can happen?"

Your Maverick also explores questions like, "What can I learn if things don't go as planned?" It doesn't get stuck searching and spinning, looking for a "why?" Rather, it surfaces an energetic "why not?"

Headamentals: Balance Best- and Worst-Case Scenarios

Take a few minutes and reflect on some recent examples of times you fell prey to an amygdala hijack. Put yourself back in these situations to consider the best- and worst-case scenarios. Just like you won't lose weight or get stronger simply by buying a gym membership, this is another area where you need to show up and do the work.

Situation 1

I recently experienced this amygdala hijack. Here's what happened:

_____

_____

What was the *worst* thing that could have happened if your Monster had taken the lead?

_____

_____

What was the *best* thing that could have happened if you had let your Maverick take the lead?

_____

_____

Situation 2

I recently experienced another amygdala hijack. Here's what happened:

_____

_____

What was the *worst* thing that could have happened if your Monster had taken the lead?

_____

_____

What was the *best* thing that could have happened if you had let your Maverick take the lead?

_____

_____

Challenges are inevitable. How you perceive and approach them makes all the difference.

Situation 3

I recently experienced a third amygdala hijack. Here's what happened:

_____

_____

What was the *worst* thing that could have happened if your Monster had taken the lead?

_____

_____

What was the *best* thing that could have happened if you had let your Maverick take the lead?

_____

_____

Yes, You Can

Ryan finds himself in Canada from time to time. His trips north of the border started when he was hired to keynote for a Canadian retailer, Princess Auto, a DIYer's best friend. Founded in 1933 and headquartered in Winnipeg, Manitoba, the company operates over fifty-five stores across Canada, serving a diverse customer base that includes mechanics, trade professionals, and home project enthusiasts. Its consistent growth, reflected in its expanding workforce of over three thousand team members, is driven by a commitment to offering unique products and a customer-focused shopping experience.

During the pandemic, Princess Auto was deemed essential by the Government of Canada. The company executives decided to say yes to helping their customers out, even if what the customers wanted wasn't part of their core business. In his recent keynote to 150 Princess Auto leaders, Ryan's big reveal was that "Princess Auto is Canada's 'can do' company." In fact, they are in the business of *Can*.

On the flip side is the one word Princess Auto will not utter: *Can't*.

Your Maverick mindset doesn't consider *Can't* first. It has no use for *Can't*. You are not inadequate, weak, inept, or wrong in any way if negative narratives run through your head. We all have these thoughts. A person's inner dialogue consists of thousands of interactions over the course of their life, and nobody has control over who raises us, who shapes us, and who we interact with. Nor can we put a stranglehold on what bubbles to the surface in our minds. But we can control how much time we spend dissecting these chronicles. Some of us simply learn to disrupt, rethink, and challenge these stories sooner than others do.

> **MAVERICK PRO TIP**
>
> Ask your Monster, "Why do you keep bringing up *Can't?*" Truly observe and audit this answer. Can you get to the root of this *Can't*?

In fact, here's a challenge for you: Every time your Monster brings forward a *Can't*, immediately switch to your Maverick, who will suggest a *Can*.

Flip "I can't seem to get that promotion" to "Hey, Monster, let's talk about what I can control to win the promotion."

Flip "I'm afraid I won't be asked to lead the new high-profile team I've been invited to join" to "Hey, Monster, let's focus on the knowledge and experience I can bring to that role and how I can demonstrate my skills in our first meeting."

Flip "My business unit can't achieve the daunting targets we've been given" to "Hey, Monster, I'm going to schedule an in-person strategy session so we can put our heads together and figure out how to make it happen."

Challenges are inevitable. How you perceive and approach them makes all the difference in the outcome. When your Monster dwells on your limitations, you develop mental barriers that prevent you from recognizing the prospects within your grasp. Your Monster creates self-fulfilling prophecies of failure.

By embracing a mindset of possibility, you can overcome obstacles, unlock potential, and inspire others to do the same. Focusing on what you can do opens doors to endless opportunities. It empowers you to act, be creative, and lean in to the resilience everyone possesses.

Headamentals: Flip the Switch

For the next few days, every time you catch your Monster telling you that you can't do something, write it down. Then invite your Maverick to look that *Can't* in the eye and tell your Monster to explain what you *Can* do. Record your thoughts here.

Situation 1
I challenged my first Monster *Can't*:
_____
_____

With a powerful Maverick *Can*:
_____
_____

Situation 2
I challenged my second Monster *Can't*:
_____
_____

With another powerful Maverick *Can*:
_____
_____

Situation 3
I challenged my third Monster *Can't*:
_____
_____

With another powerful Maverick *Can*:
_____
_____

The amygdala hijack served a useful purpose thousands of years ago when the threat of wild animals lay just beyond the campfire. It gave us an important edge in staying alive. Today, your amygdala comes in handy when you're in the path of a hurricane or a gang fight, but on a day-to-day basis, this powerful danger detector is simply inviting your Monster to join the party. And it's a party you'd be better off avoiding. When you sense your amygdala stirring up trouble, call on your Maverick to short-circuit the alarm bells and choose a more calming, productive path forward.

7
Overthinking

Overthinking, also best known as creating problems that are never there.

DAVID SIKHOSANA

YOU'RE LYING in bed, staring at the ceiling. Agonizing over an email you sent to one of your most important clients. Worrying about how your employee will receive his "Needs Improvement" performance assessment you're delivering tomorrow. Replaying a conversation from yesterday, second-guessing every word, every gesture, wondering if you said the right thing. Before you know it, it's 3 a.m., and you're wide awake, exhausted from the mental gymnastics. Welcome to the world of overthinking. We've all been there.

Nicole Ayers is a highly accomplished business unit lead at General Mills, managing their pet brands. Her elevated position comes with significant stress and a sense of isolation common among leaders. Nicole refers to her overthinking self-talk as entering "the tunnel." She explains, "I was stuck between having a lot of experience and trying to reconcile that with things changing so fast that I questioned everything: decisions I made, how I led, how I showed up for my team, and how people interpreted what I said. It was exhausting! 'The tunnel' was when I felt I could do nothing right."

Fortunately, Nicole didn't let her derailed Monster take control. She overcame her overthinking by doing something many leaders neglect to. She enlisted a few trusted team members to join the conversation. "I was lucky to have people I worked with to talk to about it and give me perspective, which is hard to have in a tunnel. Those relationships I built within my work environment really paid off because I had trusted people around me."

When leaders forge new paths in business, it often feels like navigating a dark tunnel alone without a GPS. The tunnel becomes less daunting when you can put the high beams on the problem with the help of trusted colleagues. Looking back on her self-reflective tunnel experience, Nicole shared that after exiting the tunnel, she realized she could have benefited from an even broader perspective by reaching out beyond her General Mills network to include external colleagues and mentors. "My lesson was to remember that the dark tunnel had an end, and to leverage your broader network to give you a better perspective."

> **MAVERICK PRO TIP**
>
> Who in your immediate work environment can you tap to shine the light in your tunnel? Who do you know outside of your workplace that can offer you a new or different perspective? The isolating wormhole of tunnel thinking becomes less claustrophobic when you allow others to help you think through problems you've been over-marinating.

Many of us are plagued by endless torrents of negative thoughts and emotions, often triggered by something as fleeting as a sarcastic remark from a friend, relative, or coworker. These thoughts and emotions can be a formidable enemy of productivity and well-being.

According to University of Michigan psychology professor Susan Nolen-Hoeksema, overthinking is a national epidemic among young and middle-aged adults. She found that:

- 73 percent of 25-to-35-year-olds overthink.
- Among 45-to-55-year-olds, the percentage drops to 52.
- Just 20 percent of 65-to-75-year-olds are prone to overthinking.
- Finally, women are more likely than men to be immobilized by overthinking: 57 percent of women are affected compared to 43 percent of men.

Consider the advice of Ryan's friend Kelly. She told him, "I have autism. High on the spectrum; however, my brain is wired to review every single conversation several times. Naturally, not in a positive way. You can 'coach' those intrusive thoughts into positive criticism, but it takes a lot of therapy, time, and experience." Kelly found that self-coaching was an effective antidote for ruminating, and we applaud her for putting in the work.

Overthinking is the brain's way of trying to regain control. We imagine that by thoroughly analyzing every detail, we can prepare for every possible outcome and avoid having a similarly disastrous fill-in-the-blank in the future. Sadly, rather than resulting in better decisions, overthinking is more likely to lead to increased stress and a propensity to burnout.

The Source

Overthinking stems from various factors. At its core, it's linked to the anxiety associated with fear of failure, exacerbated by our all-too-human desire for control. We imagine we can prevent negative outcomes by assessing every possible roadblock. While we don't advocate making decisions without thoughtful analysis and deliberation, overthinking tends to amplify anxiety and cloud our judgment.

While most of us overthink things now and again, leaders are particularly prone to overanalyzing, especially when they're in a new role. As people rise through the ranks, the pressure to make the right call intensifies, and those who suffer from self-doubt often struggle to make decisions. They buy time by endlessly reviewing their options, and the people they lead tend to see this as a sign of insecurity rather than a strength.

Some leaders overthink because they feel the need to prove their intelligence and demonstrate their worth and value. They end up second-guessing their initial judgments, which is time-consuming and counterproductive. Other leaders overthink because they expect to be successful in everything they do. This makes it hard for them to let go of projects or strategies that aren't working. They spend an inordinate amount of time looking for ways to make failing projects succeed instead of cutting their losses and moving on.

It's important for leaders to recognize when they're overthinking and learn to trust their instincts, make decisions with the information available, and move forward without getting bogged down in endless deliberation.

The High Cost

Overthinking leads to paralysis. Instead of taking action, we get stuck in a loop of what-ifs and hypothetical scenarios, which delays decision-making and leads to missed opportunities. It's also a huge drain on our productivity and overall well-being.

Overthinking is particularly detrimental in professional settings where the stakes are high and the desire to succeed leads to constant self-scrutiny. Too many leaders fall into the trap of analysis paralysis, and their fear of making a wrong decision leads to making no decision at all.

In addition to stalling progress, overthinking undermines a leader's self-confidence and the confidence of others, creating an atmosphere of doubt and indecision. It's important to gather relevant information and consider your options, but it's equally important to act decisively.

Consider Mark, a CEO who is highly analytical by nature. He spends an inordinate amount of time weighing the pros and cons of every business decision. While his thoroughness is admirable, his hesitancy often frustrates his team and slows the company's progress. Mark's overthinking has become a bottleneck that stifles innovation and agility.

The first step to combating overthinking is to recognize it when it's happening. Here are some common signs:

Overanalyzing: You look at a problem or situation from every possible angle and get bogged down in details that aren't important to the big picture.

Rumination: You constantly relive past events, especially things that didn't go well—a presentation, a disagreement with a colleague, or a difficult conversation with your boss.

Indecisiveness: You find it difficult to make decisions, no matter how small.

Future tripping: You're consumed with worrying about what lies ahead to the point that it holds you back. Uncertainty about what might happen, the potential for failure, and fear of the unknown keep you from doing the job that's in front of you now.

Overthinking is a common challenge—but one you can learn to manage.

Headamentals: Strategies to Overcome Overthinking

Here are some strategies leaders can adopt when they find themselves prone to overthinking:

Set clear deadlines for decisions: This creates a sense of urgency and prevents endless deliberation.

Delegate effectively: Trust your team and delegate tasks and decisions appropriately. This not only reduces your own cognitive load, but also empowers others and builds their confidence. Trusting others' expertise prevents you from overanalyzing every detail.

Focus on what's actionable: Concentrate on the steps you can take rather than getting lost in hypotheticals.

Simplify the problem: Break it down into smaller, more manageable parts to avoid feeling overwhelmed.

Trust your intuition: Your gut feeling is often the synthesis of your experiences and can guide you effectively.

Seek diverse perspectives: Diverse perspectives provide new insights and reduce the burden of finding the perfect solution. Collaborative decision-making also fosters a sense of shared responsibility.

Embrace the idea that action creates understanding: Once you've got enough information to get started, take action and learn from the outcome. This iterative process is much more effective than trying to predict every possible scenario.

Reflect on past successes: Remind yourself of times when you made good decisions with limited information. This builds confidence in your ability to do it again.

Overthinking is a common challenge, but much like the other cognitive roadblocks your Monster throws in your path, it's one you can learn to manage. The goal isn't to eliminate deep thinking, it's to prevent you from spiraling into an unproductive, isolated tunnel. Remember, leadership is about making the best decisions with the information available, not about having all the answers.

 Curious to know more about what fuels your Monster? Here are some resources to help you fight back.

CHECK YOURSELF CHECKPOINT

Congratulations! You've just reached the end of Part One of *Headamentals*. Getting yourself through the gauntlet of your own mind is no small feat.

If this first part of *Headamentals* felt like holding up a mirror to your inner critic, you're not alone. In fact, you've just joined an elite club of readers who were brave enough to confront their inner Monsters head-on. Before we move on, let's take a quick second to review and acknowledge the mental marathon you just conquered, which includes jumping multiple cognitive hurdles.

Remember when you read about impostor syndrome and thought, "Oh no. That's me!" Or when the descriptions of self-handicapping, confirmation bias, experiential avoidance, amygdala hijacks, and overthinking felt like they were ripped straight from your daily mental gymnastics routine? As you've now gathered, the concepts covered in Part One are universal human struggles.

Here's the plot twist: recognizing these mental traps isn't just a party trick. It's the first step in rewiring your brain for success. Those *Headamentals* exercises? They're not just feel-good fluff. They're cognitive calisthenics designed to build your mental muscles so you can effectively confront your Monster.

In Part Two, we'll give you a simple process to amplify your inner Maverick and manage your Monster: our 3-C Maverick Method.

If you're ready to conquer your self-talk, the next few chapters can help you become the confident leader you were meant to be.

PART TWO

The Process
The 3-C Maverick Method

The Cognitive Reframe Game

Whether you think you can or think you can't, you're right.

HENRY FORD

IMAGINE TAKING ON the daunting challenge of writing a book. Though we're authorities on the topics of accountability, leadership, corporate transformation, effective communication, strategic planning, and courageous action, each of the three of us had moments where we sparred with our own Monsters as we took on this mountain of an assignment. Over the last two years, we heard our own Monsters in unique ways.

Did you go to graduate school for six years? No? Are you a PhD? No? Then what makes you qualified to ink a book on this topic? (Suzy did go to graduate school for six years and she does have a PhD from Columbia University.)

Have you written a book before? No? You don't have the first clue about what you're doing. (Rhett and Ryan have both written books before.)

Think you are a decent writer? Think this will be a page-turner? Says who? You are going to need a lot of outside help to shape this text into anything closely resembling a book. (All three of us are decent writers.)

Despite our individual and collective accomplishments, the Monster knows the effectiveness of a solo sneak attack. Our Monsters came for us hard throughout the writing of this book because we're human, and humans are imperfect.

Now, let's talk about you.

Have you ever made a mistake, gotten in trouble, or chosen the wrong path? Sure you have. We all have. Have you ever heard your Monster chime in soon after to remind you of your mistake? Again, that's an affirmative. Most of us fall into the habit of mentally and verbally beating ourselves up instead of being gracious to ourselves and taking the opportunity to learn from our miscalculations.

You would never treat a beloved friend the way you treat yourself. It would hurt and demotivate them, and they might come to resent you or even dislike you. So why do you speak to yourself this way? When your daily thoughts are flooded with negative messages, at one point or another, you inadvertently derail yourself—maybe even hate yourself.

Many of us pay attention to negative narratives about ourselves more often than we realize. And we're here to tell you that they rarely add any value. While some of you may use this tactic as a harmless "chip on the shoulder," most of the time, talking to ourselves this way only makes us feel worse. It robs us of the opportunity to build confidence by rising up, learning to cope, and doing better next time.

We believe the path to becoming more productive and effective is realizing that you are, in fact, both your Monster and your Maverick. Managing these two realities takes discipline, awareness, and practice, but we'll give you the tools to spot and defang debilitating self-talk in your mind.

Remember, your Monster is right there in the car beside you for the long haul. Whether you like it or not, you don't have the luxury of pulling over to the side of the road and telling your Monster to take a hike. Knowing it's along for the ride, keep it safely buckled in the back seat instead of allowing it to drive or ride shotgun.

The way to keep the Monster in its right place is to reframe the conversation in your mind. This can be achieved by utilizing something we call our 3-C Maverick Method, which positions your Maverick—not your Monster—in the copilot seat. Please note: This is not about shunning your Monster. It's about ensuring the Monster doesn't get control of the wheel. It will teach you how to listen more closely to your Maverick so you can get where you're trying to go. There's no time to waste, so put the car in drive.

Catch, Confront, and Change It

Our 3-C Maverick Method is modeled on well-established psychological research and designed to help you Catch, Confront, and Change negative thought patterns, emotions, and behaviors as they occur. It works like this:

Catch It: Recognize when you're spiraling into destructive self-talk and identify the negative thoughts swirling around in your head.

Confront It: Examine the source of the unproductive messages you're telling yourself and confront them head-on to figure out if they're true.

Change It: Generate alternative narratives that are more realistic than the negative stories you've spent a lifetime perfecting.

The reframe game is also known as cognitive reframing, developed in the 1960s by Aaron Beck, PhD, a professor of psychiatry at the University of Pennsylvania and the father of cognitive behavioral therapy (CBT). It is Beck's work that led to our 3-C Maverick Method. CBT is based on the idea that how you *think* about a situation impacts how you *feel* about it, which shapes how you *act*. Grounded in Stoic philosophy, it teaches you that although you can't control your reality, you can control how you think about it and how you behave in response.

Here's a simple example of cognitive reframing we can all relate to. You're scrolling through your Instagram feed one evening and see that three of your work colleagues went out for dinner without you. Your initial thought is, "I guess they don't like me." Then, you take it a step further. You think, "Gosh, I don't have any friends at work. There must be something fundamentally wrong with me."

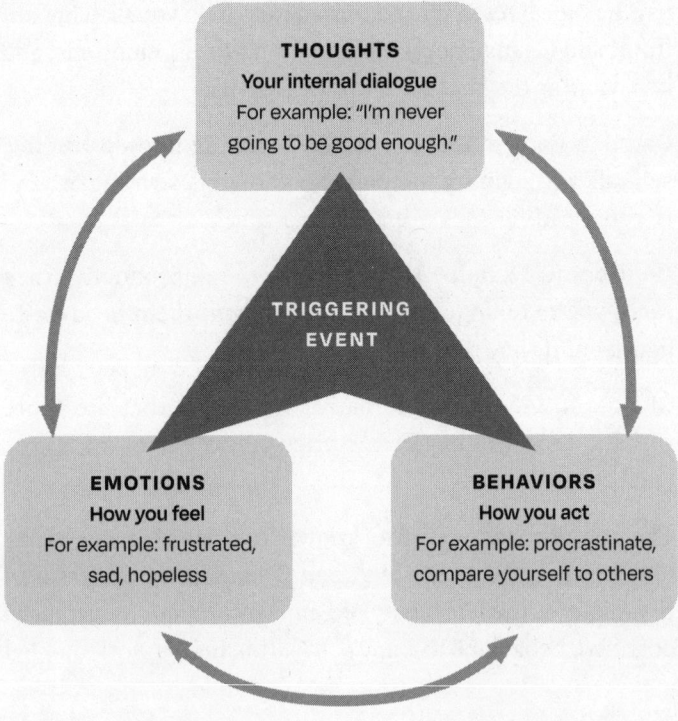

These spiraling thoughts trigger feelings of rejection, isolation, and sorrow. Now what? Instead of wallowing in those emotions or surrendering to them, when you slow down and identify them, you've taken the first crucial step. You've caught the thoughts and feelings.

Upon further reflection, you think: "They're working on a project together and they're probably talking about it. *I'm making this more personal than it needs to be.*" You realize there's solid evidence that doesn't support your initial discouraging thoughts. In fact, your colleagues have invited you to go out with them before, and they often tell you how much they enjoy being with you. By acknowledging real behavior patterns and asking questions, you are actively confronting your negative thoughts and feelings.

Still chewing on that dumb Instagram post, you notice that a few other members of your work tribe are missing from the photo. The fact that they even posted the photo shows they meant no harm. If the group were being strategically discreet, they wouldn't have posted the picture at all! "Let's be real," you tell yourself, "I don't have to be invited to every event or dinner, just as I would not invite them to every function I attend."

Voila! You've successfully changed the narrative with the help of your composed Maverick. Instead of walking into work the next day with a big resentful chip on your shoulder, you've successfully tamed and reframed the Monster through the 3-C Maverick Method. By doing so, your anxiety dissipates, and your mind is freed up to focus on something more productive.

As humans, we are creatures of habit, and we find comfort in routine behaviors, even when they don't serve us well. Chances are your negative thoughts are deeply ingrained, but you can learn to consciously and deliberately "let go" to break free from these harmful patterns with the intent of forging a more productive path forward.

Although our minds often resist change, our 3-C Maverick Method capitalizes on the brain's inherent plasticity—the capacity to rewire itself through learning and experience. By consciously redirecting our thoughts, actions, and reactions toward healthier choices, we gradually forge new neural pathways that bolster our emotional resilience and mental agility.

Substitution is at the heart of redirection. Your habits are like well-worn trails through a dense forest. To forge a new direction, you must intentionally veer off the old path and set a new course. That requires both self-awareness and a commitment to replacing old narratives and behaviors with new, more positive ones. For instance, if stress triggers the urge to scarf down a pint of your favorite ice cream, redirecting to a replacement behavior entails a few minutes of conscious focus. In greater detail, here's how to use the 3-Cs to reframe your brain.

Step 1: Catch It Start by developing the habit of recognizing when you're filling your mind with negative messages. Use your emotions as cues. When you feel a knot in your stomach or your shoulders tightening, pause and try to figure out if your Monster has taken the wheel. If you notice your heart is beating faster or find yourself jiggling your foot, what self-defeating thoughts are at play? Take the time to identify them.

Step 2: Confront It Make the space to understand the origin of your negative self-talk and the circumstances that trigger it. Ask yourself: "Is what I'm thinking true? What evidence do I have to back it up? What function does it serve?" This is one of the harder parts of the process because you have to proactively confront your thinking with evidence: facts, situations, or statements that dispute your negative self-talk.

Step 3: Change It Based on what you learn when you confront your negative thoughts, you can identify more realistic and positive alternative messages to replace your self-critical thoughts. This is flexing that mindset muscle that always benefits from a good lift. For example, if you're thinking "I'm a failure," you might replace that thought with "I've had setbacks in the past, but I've also had successes. I'm capable of learning from my mistakes and moving forward."

In the chapters ahead, we'll crack open each of the 3-C steps in more detail and give you a chance to reflect on situations that can be viewed through a different, more positive lens.

Catch It

The most dangerous lies are the ones we tell ourselves.

UNKNOWN

YOU KNOW that space between being asleep and awake? It's a vulnerable time for most of us. Some of us get lucky by remaining in a heavenly dream state. You've been whisked away to a memory you relish from your past or a fictitious storyline that makes you smile. Others of us have slipped into a calamitous nightmare. Instead of thinking happy thoughts, our Monster is quietly pulling the strings behind the scenes, making us feel anxious, sad, or even distraught about something real or unreal.

The first step to dealing with a negative narrative is to Catch It in the act. Some people are so used to scolding themselves for every little thing they do "wrong" that they don't even notice they're doing it. But you can learn to notice. And until you do, the same story will repeat itself in an endless loop.

If you never learn how to identify negative feedback loops, you might feel as if you are living in an interminable *Twilight Zone* episode starring yourself. It's a rerun that's hard to shake.

Your Monster gives you physiological cues to alert you that it's on your doorstep. Ryan feels tension in his neck and shoulders. Suzy's gut tightens. Rhett's signal is the onset of a mild headache.

Headamentals: How Does Your Monster Show Up?

Although we have only one Monster inhabiting our minds, each of our Monsters can show up differently depending on our moods. Let's start by spending a few minutes reflecting on which aspect of your Monster shows up most frequently for you. Please don't skip this. Remember, it takes hard work to catch the Monster in your mind.

Monster 1
Think of a time when your Monster recently showed up:

_____

_____

What triggered this Monster's appearance?

_____

_____

What is the source of these Monster thoughts?

_____

_____

I can tell my Monster is about to surface because I feel:

_____

_____

Monster 2
Another version of my Monster that shows up frequently is:

_____

_____

What triggers this Monster's appearance?
_____
_____

What is the source of these Monster thoughts?
_____
_____

I can tell my Monster is about to surface because I feel:
_____
_____

Monster 3
Another version of my Monster that shows up frequently is:
_____
_____

What triggers this Monster's appearance?
_____
_____

What is the source of these Monster thoughts?
_____
_____

I can tell my Monster is about to surface because I feel:
_____
_____

To grow, it's essential to build on past successes and learn from your failures.

You've just identified several versions of your Monster. Great work! Sometimes, it's about creating a new process to short-circuit the autopilot tendencies we defer to. To break those patterns in the future, here are some tools to help Catch It.

Catch It Journaling

They say that a short pencil is stronger than the longest memory. Writing something down makes a deeper impression than simply thinking about it. Known as the encoding or generation effect, it's a psychological phenomenon that helps you remember the information you actively generate better than the information you passively read or receive. When you write something down, you're actively producing information, which encodes it in your memory.

Starting a Catch It Journal gives you a place to collect and reflect on your thoughts so you can replace the negative ones with positive ones in real time. Journaling also helps you identify patterns in your negative self-talk so you can understand and confront the beliefs that are holding you back.

Recording just how often we belittle ourselves and the language we use to do it is a powerful exercise. Chances are you'd never speak to anyone you work with, care for, or love that way. In fact, you probably wouldn't even speak to someone you don't like that way.

Here are some prompts to get started:

- When you're having a bad day, what are some of the negative thoughts that take up space in your brain?
- What's the source of these judgments and feelings?
- What triggers them? Do they occur when you are in a particular environment (at home or at work) or around a particular person (or people)?

> **MAVERICK PRO TIP**
>
> Buy a notebook or open a Google Doc to use for your Catch It Journal and start using it today. Starting small is the call.

Throughout the course of the day, take notes on your phone or in a small notebook when you find yourself dwelling on something that's working against you. To expedite the process, take a video selfie to capture the negative self-talk you're experiencing. Now, study the video clip. What did you learn about yourself? Jot down your detective notes in your journal.

Whatever medium you choose to use, a Catch It Journal will help you recognize when your Monster is trying to bring out the worst version of yourself, acting as your own enemy and thwarting your growth as an individual and as a professional. It doesn't take a lot of time, and your efforts will be repaid tenfold in the long run.

This practice shouldn't take over your life. Spending five or ten minutes a day on self-reflection is fundamental training. So, take your mind to the mental gym; you don't even have to stay for very long. And commit to writing in your Catch It Journal regularly. It will put you on the path to developing those "Catch It" muscles. It will also enhance your mental clarity and give you a direction to work toward. It reminds you of what you've been through, fueling you to go further than you've gone before.

Hold your negative self-talk up to the light and, when possible, document a more accurate version of reality. Here are a few examples:

Wednesday, 8:35 a.m.

Monster Narrative: I'm giving a talk to the CEO and her executive leadership team this afternoon, and I'm pretty sure I don't have anything to say that they want to hear. I don't understand why they want to waste their time listening to me.

Maverick Reframe: That's not accurate. This is the second time they've asked me to share the work I'm doing. They must find it valuable.

Thursday, 3:15 p.m.

Monster Narrative: I'm disappointed that I haven't drafted our team's communications plan yet. I understand the importance of communicating what we're doing to the wider organization, and I take full responsibility for failing on this one.

Maverick Reframe: That thought isn't helpful. I'll finalize the communications plan next week and make sure we don't skip a beat going forward. I'm not a failure at all. We run at a fast pace, and it's not easy to find time to create things like this.

Friday, 6:15 p.m.

Monster Narrative: Phew! I can put another week behind me. It was a long hard slog, but I made it! Three presentations in four days is a lot, and sadly, they weren't that great. Why can't I discipline myself to do a better job preparing for each one? They're important.

Maverick Reframe: That thought isn't accurate. The feedback from every audience was positive overall. Based on the reactions in the room, I think I can make future presentations even more compelling, and I will!

In the meantime, use this space to practice writing an entry:

_____
_____
_____
_____
_____
_____

Wasn't that easy?

Spend a few minutes reflecting on the benefits of keeping a Catch It Journal.

_____
_____

What might get in the way of writing faithfully in your Catch It Journal?

_____
_____
_____

What can you do to make writing in your Catch It Journal a habit?

_____
_____
_____

Keep it simple.

Try to capture your Monster narratives as they happen, and don't stop there. Take the time to immediately reframe your mindset through a curious, optimistic lens. Writing about endless possibilities for growth with an upbeat tone is far more effective than writing about what went wrong in a timid, uncreative, "meh" voice.

Your Catch It Journal is a way to track your progress from past Derailed You to future Determined You. By committing to recording your goals and achievements as well as your challenges, you can literally spot the moments you'll want to repeat. To grow, it's essential to build on past successes and learn from your failures. And that's only possible when you spot them and remember them.

As Carol Kauffman, Harvard Medical School professor and the founder of the Institute of Coaching, wisely observed, "Failure is forgetting."

Building the Practice

Be patient with yourself, and over time, journaling will become a positive part of your daily routine. Here are some helpful tips to get started:

Start small: Document your Monster narratives with just a few words, gradually increasing the detail of your journal entries as you get into the swing of things.

Set realistic goals: Commit to writing in your Catch It Journal just once a day. As you begin to see how it's helping you quiet your Monster, you can increase the frequency.

Create a plan: Ideally, you'll write in your Catch It Journal as soon as you realize your Monster has made an unwelcome appearance, but if not, make a mental note to record an entry before you call it a day.

Schedule it: Put ten minutes (to start) of journaling in your calendar at the same time every day. By having this on your calendar, you let technology work for you, and you'll be more consistent.

Hold yourself accountable: At the end of the week, review the number of days you made at least one entry. If you haven't maintained a steady pace, find an accountability partner to keep you motivated on the days when you struggle to maintain your commitment to be proactive.

Focus on the benefits: Notice any changes in your mood, responses, and behaviors once you've developed a journaling habit.

Celebrate your successes: No matter how small the successes, make time to celebrate them along the way. This will help keep you motivated and reinforce the habit.

Commit to sixty days: This is the minimum amount of time it takes to make a habit automatic. Once you make it through the initial conditioning phase, writing in your Catch It Journal will be much easier to sustain. If it's not working for you, let it go, but withhold judgment until at least two months have passed.

Daily Catch It alarms are a way of practicing momentary time sampling, a tool used in behavioral observation. It's a way to check in with yourself during the day to see who's in charge. Is it your Monster or your Maverick? Which self-talk are you heeding?

Rhett knows it's easy to get off track and let others alter his day and his mood. He uses the alarm on his phone as a trigger to short-circuit negativity and prevent his Monster from renting too much space in his head. Suzy's watch alarm reminds her to check on her mental and physical stress throughout the day. She takes a minute to check in on her Monster to improve her focus when she returns to work. Ryan sets alarms on his phone to ensure his behavior aligns with his values and personal purpose. He then does a quick audit to see if he's on track to achieve his goals and runs a temperature check on how his values are influencing his decision-making.

> **MAVERICK PRO TIP**
>
> It takes a village. If you are worried about personal accountability, go to our website to join our private Headamentals group to find others who are committed to keeping a Catch It Journal (headamentals.com/mavericks).

There is no shortage of hacks and tricks to help Catch your Monster in action and make it part of your daily routine. Like any other habit we set out to build, the Catch It practice can easily become your default with a little self-awareness, diligence, and commitment. When we pause to reflect on the constant stream of narratives running in our minds, we are better equipped to Confront and Change them.

10
Confront It

The important thing is not to stop questioning. Curiosity has its own reason for existing.

ALBERT EINSTEIN

THE VOICE of reason. She talks to us regularly, helping us make relatively complex decisions quickly. *Do I have time to go for a quick run, take a shower, make breakfast, and get dressed before my Zoom call in fifty minutes?* Then there's that other voice—the voice that's unreasonable. *If I don't fit a run in this morning, I am a certifiable failure.* These two voices, as we know by now, duel it out in our minds all day like squabbling siblings who need to be sent to their rooms.

Once you learn how to spot your inner bullies, as you did in the Catch It phase of the 3-C Maverick Method, it can be tempting to go full ostrich and bury your head in the sand. We know how difficult it is to sit with uncomfortable thoughts when they arise. We also know this struggle can lead to more damaging internal dialogue, such as: *Why can't I stop thinking this way? Am I really this weak?*

Learning to Confront negative self-talk thoughtfully involves asking yourself if the messages you're telling yourself are really true and searching for evidence to support them if they exist.

Gather Evidence by Asking the Right Questions

Today, ChatGPT is all the rage. Like a personal assistant, AI platforms are exceptional tools to efficiently gather information. It all comes down to prompting ChatGPT with the right questions. The success of the quest is in the question! Gathering evidence on your own thoughts is no different. It all comes down to asking the right questions.

Getting to the root of Monster thinking is an effective way to short-circuit a behavior you'd like to eliminate. Once you catch yourself having destructive thoughts, step back and consider where they're coming from rather than trying to suppress them. Sure, hostile thoughts threaten your sense of self, but managing negative self-talk involves learning how to deconstruct and brave difficult feelings. This means summoning the courage and creating the space to face yourself.

Let's examine the power of asking the right questions. When you hear or see a question, your mind automatically tries to answer it. So, if you're feeling cynical or pessimistic, instead of staying open-minded or relying on a hollow "look on the bright side," ask yourself questions that will enable you to pivot, learn, and do better next time.

Consider the two common situations that follow, as well as some questions that will help you replace critical thoughts with productive actions and considerations for the future.

Your boss just chewed you out for missing a project deadline. Instead of telling yourself that you're a failure or thinking your boss will hold it against you forever, ask yourself:

What can I learn so this doesn't happen again?

_____

_____

What can I tell my boss to help her regain confidence in my ability to deliver?

_____

_____

Who can I collaborate with to produce better outputs moving forward?

_____

How might I better shape my future communication to ensure all parties know where I stand on a project?

_____

_____

Why did I miss the deadline in the first place?

_____

_____

Does missing one deadline make me a failure?

_____

_____

What's a more accurate way to think about it?

_____

_____

You didn't communicate an urgent company message clearly and promptly. Rather than telling yourself you don't deserve to be a team leader, ask yourself:

What prevented me from communicating this announcement quickly and clearly?

_____

_____

_____

Why did I think other tasks took priority over this one?

_____

_____

_____

What can I tell my team about how I plan to communicate messages like this in the future?

_____

_____

_____

Who can I call on to be a mock audience for future messages to be sure they're clear and on point?

_____

_____

Why do I think that messing up one company message means I'm unfit to lead a team?

_____

_____

_____

Getting to the root of Monster thinking is an effective way to short-circuit a behavior you'd like to eliminate.

Eventually, whatever is bothering you—a dark mood or an actual situation—will shift when you Confront It with the right questions.

Michael Smith, vice president of marketing at PepsiCo, was very frank with us about how he handles self-talk through a rigorous questioning process. He said, "When funneled positively, self-talk can lead to more strategic rigor before making decisions, but when allowed to spiral negatively, it can erode confidence and undermine leadership ability. I attempt to channel it toward the analysis of a problem or challenge that ends in a simplified way forward and clear next steps. When structured in this manner, self-talk can provide clarity and increased confidence."

Michael shared his own Confront It strategy: "My trick is to go back to the beginning. Why did you start the project? What were you trying to accomplish? Try to forget all the other elements clouding your vision, spinning you in circles, and leaving you lost. This decluttering of the mind helps me re-engage the most important questions."

There you have it.

Headamentals: Find Future Lessons in Past Mistakes

Following the scenario-and-reframe model laid out in the previous two examples, take a few minutes to identify situations where you missed the mark. What messages did you tell yourself, and what questions could reframe your negative self-talk into lessons for the future?

Describe Situation 1

_____
_____
_____

What messages did you tell yourself?

_____
_____
_____

What questions could reframe those messages into lessons for the future?

_____
_____
_____

Describe Situation 2

_____
_____
_____

What messages did you tell yourself?

_____
_____
_____

What questions could reframe those messages into lessons for the future?

_____

_____

_____

Describe Situation 3

_____

_____

_____

What messages did you tell yourself?

_____

_____

_____

What questions could reframe those messages into lessons for the future?

_____

_____

_____

After you get a sense of your inner Monster's messages, take a few deep breaths so you can de-escalate the spiral and take stock of what has led to your negative self-perception. Ask yourself the following questions and write down your answers:

What story am I telling myself?
_____
_____
_____

Is this story based on emotions or facts?
_____

Is there evidence to support it, or is it just my negative self-talk?
_____
_____

Is it derailing me or making me determined?
_____
_____

Is it giving me energy or sapping my strength?
_____
_____

What messages can I replace this story with that are more useful?
_____
_____
_____

Asking the right questions to gather evidence has two important built-in elements for growth. First, your brain finds joy in pondering a challenging puzzle, so it will try to answer a question without much conscious effort. Second, continuous improvement is always possible if you allow yourself to accept opportunities for growth as they present themselves.

Instead of allowing your Monster to muster up the "I'm a failure" tale, allow your Maverick to see the moment for what it is—another life experiment and learning opportunity so you can do better the next time. Focusing your attention on what you learned will calm your Monster while your Maverick figures out how to frame things differently.

If you find yourself perpetually, hopelessly (so it seems) stuck in the Monster state, don't stress. The magical Change It process shows you how to generate alternate, positive thoughts to replace the untrue stories your Monster is telling you.

Change It

Believe you can, and you're halfway there.

THEODORE ROOSEVELT

YOU'VE LEARNED to successfully Catch a nasty narrative you've been telling yourself. You've gathered evidence around your negative self-talk, and you've learned how to ask questions to Confront It. Now, we'll help you develop strategies to Change It to a purposeful, productive, action-oriented thought. Instead of focusing on the negatives, look for positive opportunities for growth. For example, instead of thinking "I can't do this," change the narrative to "I haven't done this yet, but I can learn."

Headamentals: Change the Story

Once you catch your Monster trying to take the steering wheel of your mind, put in the hard work to change what it is telling you. Reflect on the situations you identified in Chapter 9: "Catch It." How can you flip the switch on your Monster by interjecting your Maverick?

Monster Message 1:

_____

_____

_____

Maverick Change:

_____
_____
_____

Monster Message 2:

_____
_____
_____

Maverick Change:

_____
_____
_____

Monster Message 3:

_____
_____
_____

Maverick Change:

_____
_____
_____

One of the biggest challenges of putting your Monster where it belongs is overcoming the tendency to ruminate on the negative messages we tell ourselves. And they pop up pretty much anytime: when you're sitting down to a meal, listening to a podcast, talking with friends, and worst of all, when you're trying to fall asleep. But until you can stop them from spinning in your head, it's almost impossible to move past them, let alone change them.

One of the "letting go" hacks Ryan shares with his son is to imagine his body is like a boat. If water penetrates the hull, what happens to that boat? It sinks. Negative thoughts work like water. They can sink our boats if we're not careful. Your Maverick has to work hard to make sure your Monster doesn't send you to the bottom of the ocean.

Two Monks

From boats to Buddhism, the lesson of the two monks will likely hit home.

Once upon a time, two monks were traveling together on a long and arduous journey to a distant monastery in search of further enlightenment. Along the way, they came to a fast-flowing river with a strong current. As they prepared to cross it, they noticed a young woman standing by the water's edge. She appeared to be in distress, knowing she wouldn't be able to cross the river on her own.

As soon as she noticed the two monks, she approached them and asked for help. She explained that she needed to get to the other side of the river but was afraid of being swept away by the powerful current. Without hesitation, one of the monks immediately lifted her onto his back, carried her across the river, and gently placed her on the opposite bank.

The woman expressed her gratitude to the monk and continued on her way. The two monks resumed their journey, walking for several hours in silence. When the day drew to a close and they finally arrived at their destination, the second monk spoke in a tone of disbelief and concern. He said to his companion, "Brother, we have taken a vow of celibacy, and we are not to ever touch a woman. Yet you carried that woman across the river!"

The monk who helped the woman smiled and replied, "Brother, I put her down on the other side of the river hours ago, but you have carried her with you all the way to the monastery."

When you find yourself repeating negative messages you've been given or told yourself, think about the energy the second monk expended by refusing to leave the woman at the river as his fellow traveler did.

Headamentals: Let It Go

Spend a few minutes reflecting on situations when you couldn't prevent the memory of an unhappy situation from playing in an endless loop.

Situation 1
What was the situation?

_____

_____

Why weren't you able to move on from your ruminations?

_____

_____

_____

What power did this event have over you?

___
___

What might your Maverick suggest now?

___
___

Spend a few minutes reflecting on another situation or two where you couldn't let something go.

Situation 2
What was the situation?

___
___

Why weren't you able to move on from your ruminations?

___
___

What power did this event have over you?

___
___

Letting go of past hurts, failures, or injustices is the ultimate way to decrease their power over you.

What might your Maverick suggest now?

___

Situation 3
What was the situation?

___

Why weren't you able to move on from your ruminations?

___

What power did this event have over you?

___

What might your Maverick suggest now?

___

Letting go of past hurts, failures, or injustices is the ultimate way to decrease their power over you. We're not saying you need to forgive and forget every past wrong, but when you take the wind out of their sails, you're making an active change in your perspective. You are changing the narrative to something better suited to where you want to go and grow today, as opposed to yesterday.

Semantics: Nix the Personal Pronouns

Susan Pitt, the director of brand experience at General Mills, shared a creative way of dealing with her Monster. She said, "We have a joke in my house where we name our negative self-talk. Mine is Steve. It's really fun to say 'shut up, Steve,' and disassociate him from one's own self or inner monologue. You sound a little crazy, but that's the fun of it. This is part of a general philosophy my husband and I have which is 'name it to tame it.' When you give something a name, it normalizes it a bit and helps you see it more objectively."

Susan's trick made us think about how we think about ourselves in our own minds. According to a 2014 study titled "Self-Talk as a Regulatory Mechanism: How You Do It Matters," published by the American Psychological Association in the *Journal of Personality and Social Psychology*, the language people use to refer to themselves affects the way they feel, think, and behave under stress. The researchers cited a 2010 interview with famed basketball player LeBron James in which he said, "I didn't [want to] make an emotional decision. I wanted to do what's best for LeBron James and to do what makes LeBron James happy."

Noting how James referred to himself in the third person during the interview, the researchers designed a study to examine whether this semantic change could help people be resilient in the face of stressful situations. Indeed, they discovered that people who referred to themselves in the third person recovered faster from social stressors, were less nervous, and performed better during interpersonal interactions. They were also able to regulate social anxiety more effectively.

Why does this work? It is often easier to believe in others than in yourself. Using your own name creates a distancing effect, allowing you to see yourself almost as another person—a capable, brilliant person who can do whatever you envision. This practice also helps you remove yourself emotionally from a negative experience, allowing you to bring more mental resources to bear on whatever you're dealing with rather than defaulting to an emotional knee-jerk reaction.

The next time you're trying to change your perception of yourself and your capabilities—whether you are crafting a verbal affirmation, writing a note to your future self in your journal, or giving yourself a pep talk before a challenging situation—give this strategy a try.

Instead of saying, "I am a brilliant, capable person who will deliver a powerful presentation today," say to yourself, "[Your name] is a brilliant, capable person who will deliver a powerful presentation today." The goal is to separate yourself from your own negative narratives. Changing how you refer to yourself and losing the "I" pronoun is an effective way to do this.

No one ever said change was easy, but flipping your internal script and seeing yourself through a different lens will bring you that much closer to permanently leaning into your Maverick's positive dialogue vs. succumbing to the toxicity of your Monster.

The 3-C Maverick Method is your Monster's worst nightmare. Here's more information about how to turn the tables—and get back in the driver's seat.

CHECK YOURSELF CHECKPOINT

You're closer than ever to *Headamentals* mastery!

Change is hard. We all know that, but you're getting there. You've learned how to identify your negative thoughts and capture them when they rear their ugly heads in your Catch It Journal. You can Confront those nasty thoughts by gathering evidence and asking the right questions. And you can take the final step in our 3-C Maverick Method to Change the narrative from negative to positive.

With the process of cognitive reframing from Part Two of this book squarely in your self-talk arsenal, we'll show you exactly how to put this process into practice by taking down five common villainous Monster Archetypes that try to sabotage your productivity. We've identified these archetypes through our extensive work with leaders like yourself, who tend to battle the same Monster messaging. Using the strategies we've used on the field of real life to turn personal performance and companies around, we'll show you how to systematically dismantle those archetypes, step into your vast potential, and retrain your brain.

Process plus Practice makes Perfect. Just kidding. The concept of Perfection is a classic Monster lie whispered in your ear to make you feel less than. Like you'll never measure up or achieve success at the levels to which you aspire. We don't believe in Perfect. We know it's a sham. We believe every business leader's number one product is productivity. And when process is put into practice, the result is enhanced productivity: for you, for your team, and for your organization.

Let's do this.

PART THREE

The Practice
Retrain Your Brain

The Big 5 Monster Archetypes

We can't always control the outcome, but all of us can try.

MARSHALL GOLDSMITH

PICTURE THIS: You're surrounded by colleagues in a bustling office, yet you feel utterly alone. Sound familiar? You're not the only one who feels this way. Despite living in the most connected era in human history, loneliness has become a modern epidemic, doubling since the 1980s.

According to Vivek Murthy, US surgeon general at the time of writing, over 40 percent of American adults report feeling lonely. Loneliness is seeping into workplaces at an alarming rate, and it's a productivity nightmare. Nearly 70 percent of first-time CEOs who experience loneliness say it negatively impacts their performance.

It's not surprising when you remember that our ancestors relied on social connections for survival. Today, that need is hardwired into our nervous system. When we're lonely, our bodies react as if we're in danger:

- Decision-making and emotional regulation suffer
- Stress hormones like cortisol spike
- Inflammation increases

It's like our brains are too busy looking for threats to focus on work. Lonely workers are five times more likely to suffer from sleep issues and one and a half times more likely to be disengaged. And this disengagement comes at a steep price:

- 16 percent lower profitability
- 37 percent higher absenteeism
- 49 percent more accidents
- 65 percent lower share price over time

Here's a shocking statistic: Loneliness reduces longevity by up to a staggering 50 percent—far outpacing more commonly recognized health risks. It's equivalent to smoking fifteen cigarettes a day.

The good news? With proper tools and training, we can turn this around.

Workplaces characterized by caring, supportive relationships lead to higher organizational performance. By fostering connection, we improve well-being, productivity, and, ultimately, the bottom line. Finding workplace harmony is the last thing your Monster dreams of. Its bottom line is to keep you isolated so it can do what it does best.

As we know, Monsters channel irrational, false, and harmful thinking patterns in your mind. These are known as cognitive distortions, and they were first identified by psychiatrist Aaron Beck, one of the most influential minds in modern psychology. Cognitive distortions are negative thought patterns about oneself, others, or the world. They are often automatic and unconscious, and they can be very difficult to change.

Beck discovered that these negative thought patterns played a key role in feeding our anxiety. But by becoming aware of them, our Maverick can learn to spot them, challenge them, and develop more productive ways of taming the irrational ways of thinking that fuel our emotional distress.

Although the concept of cognitive distortions has been around for over a half-century, the subject was never meant to be colloquial dinner table conversation. Since you're now well versed in self-conversations, it's time to give your Maverick the tools to become a competent sleuth to recognize the five cognitive distortions your Monster loves to feast on. To help you tackle these distortions, we've identified the Big 5 Monster Archetypes, or, as we also like to call them: CAMOS.

CAMOS is an acronym that is also the abbreviation for camouflage, which is fitting given that the following five cognitive distortions represented by CAMOS often conceal the truth, making it difficult to spot reality when we're shackled by a negative self-talk narrative. There are many different types of cognitive distortions, but the following five are the big ones to watch out for:

C   The Catastrophizer
A   The Always Righter
M   The Mind Reader
O   The Overgeneralizer
S   The Should-er

The power of practice is well documented in psychology and neuroscience, but this power doesn't come from simply going through the motions. Effective practice requires deliberate, consistent effort and focus.

The key to shrinking derailing self-talk starts with your ability to retrain your brain. Through repetition, your brain will create new neural pathways and strengthen existing ones, allowing you to eradicate negative thought patterns.

This is where your Headamentals training kicks into high gear. We'll delve into each of the Monster Archetypes that make up CAMOS. No doubt these big five have ponged around in your head, sabotaging your success… and now you'll have their playbook.

We've included examples for the five cognitive distortions so you can better identify how each shows up, along with how to beat them at their own game. Do you recognize, relate to, or mirror one or more of them? For each of the Headamentals, utilize the 3-C Maverick Method (Catch It, Confront It, Change It) to flip those Monster saboteurs into Maverick matadors.

> **MAVERICK PRO TIP**
>
> It's easy to first spot the behavior of a coworker or colleague through a Monster Archetype. But we hope you'll have the courage to also identify yourself within each of the archetypes below.

Monster Archetype 1: The Catastrophizer

Catastrophizers tend to immediately see the negativity in a scenario or conversation. They overindex on the "what's the worst that can happen" and expect a negative outcome, no matter how unlikely. This leads them to believe that even a simple mistake or setback will result in disaster. For example, if a work project is slightly delayed, a Catastrophizer might think, "This delay will ruin the entire project, cost the company millions, and could cost me my job." The Catastrophizer irrationally assumes a glass-half-empty scenario, which often leads to blowing a pressing situation way out of proportion.

While this mindset might serve Catastrophizers well in high-risk scenarios, their direct beeline to a worst-case mindset thwarts morale. It diminishes possibility, often leading to intense anxiety and a sense of helplessness. If they can learn to harness their exaggerated Monster impulses, they can catch themselves before those impulses adversely affect them or others.

Here are a few Catastrophizer Headamentals for your handiwork. Reframe their brains!

Catastrophizer Headamental #1

Olivia is a rising star on her team. During a team meeting, Olivia's suggestion was met with a few skeptical comments, and immediately she started to think, "My ideas are always dismissed. No one values my input. I'll never be able to contribute meaningfully here." Olivia exaggerates the reactions, ignoring the fact that constructive criticism is a normal part of team dynamics and that her contributions are often valued.

How can Olivia's Maverick help reframe this situation?

Catch It: _____
_____

Confront It: _____
_____

Change It: _____
_____

Catastrophizer Headamental #2

CEO Matt is three months into his new job, and he's about to lead his first board meeting since stepping into this role. Unfortunately, the numbers have not improved during the time he's been at the helm. To make matters worse, Matt hasn't been able to establish a strong relationship with the board chair. When he receives an email from the chairman the night before the meeting titled "Coffee in the AM—Urgent!!!," he panics. Matt begins to worry that he won't be employed by the time the board convenes. Instead of focusing on his presentation, he's now consumed with fear about what could possibly be coming in this climactic early morning coffee with the board chair.

How can Matt's Maverick help reframe this situation?

Catch It:
_____
_____

Confront It:
_____
_____

Change It:
_____
_____

Monster Archetype 2: The Always Righter

The Always Righter archetype is characterized by an unwavering belief in one's own correctness. Always Righters have a hard time acknowledging their own mistakes and refuse to consider others' viewpoints. As the name suggests, they are determined to prove they're right and everyone else is wrong. It's possible Always Righters are striving for perfection, or they're blinded by an innate fear of failure, or they're battling their own lack of self-esteem. Whatever the root, Always Righters are known for their inflexibility, their set-in-their-ways behavior, and overall fixed mindset. Reframe the Always Righter scenarios for the following Headamentals.

Always Righter Headamental #1

As SVP of strategy, Daniel sends a detailed strategy proposal to the president. When he doesn't respond immediately, instead of doubting himself, he becomes increasingly indignant. "My analysis is flawless. The president clearly doesn't

THE BIG 5 MONSTER ARCHETYPES

understand the sophistication of my approach." He sends multiple follow-up emails defending his position and highlighting his credentials. In meetings, he shuts down his colleagues' input and ideas, saying, "I've been doing this for fifteen years. Trust me, this is the only way forward." His certainty in his infallibility creates tension throughout the team and damages collaboration.

How can Daniel's Maverick help reframe this situation?

Catch It: _____

_____

Confront It: _____

_____

Change It: _____

_____

Always Righter Headamental #2

Diana, a senior marketing manager, faces criticism about her new spring campaign's messaging. Instead of considering the feedback, she produces a twenty-page document citing every reason to stick with her campaign, along with a note that includes every successful campaign she's ever run. "I've never had a failed campaign. I worry the team doesn't understand modern marketing." Diana won't attend feedback sessions, claiming they're unnecessary since her approach is obviously the best approach. Her inflexibility leads to alienation, a strained client relationship, and missed opportunities for campaign optimization.

How can Diana's Maverick help reframe this situation?

Catch It: _____

_____

Confront It: _____

_____

Change It: _____

_____

Monster Archetype 3: The Mind Reader

Mind Readers jump to conclusions and assume they know what other people are thinking, without any concrete evidence, and often to their own detriment. Mind Readers don't usually try to verify their assumptions because they're convinced they'll be negative. This erodes trust in relationships. When people assume others are harboring negative thoughts about them, they tend to become defensive and accuse others of thoughts or intentions they never had. Behaving as a Mind Reader reinforces existing negative core beliefs, such as "I'm not good enough" or "People don't like me." Every instance of this kind of Mind Reader thinking further confirms to the person that these beliefs are true, making them even more entrenched. The truth is there's no real evidence for these thoughts. Mind Readers are just interpreting situations negatively based on unfounded assumptions.

How can you help the following Mind Readers change their tune?

Mind Reader Headamental #1

Alex, a department head, is about to conduct performance reviews. He notices that one of his employees, Lisa, has been more reserved lately. He assumes that she must be upset with him, perhaps feeling unappreciated or unfairly treated. Instead of addressing these assumptions directly, Alex treads carefully around Lisa during the review and provides vague feedback, which denies Lisa the benefit of Alex's insights. In reality, Lisa has been preoccupied with personal matters and appreciates Alex's leadership, but his assumption prevents an open and productive dialogue.

How can Alex's Maverick help reframe this situation?

Catch It: _____

_____

Confront It: _____

_____

Change It: _____

_____

Mind Reader Headamental #2

Sheila is a project manager at a midsize marketing firm where she leads a high-stakes campaign for a major client. One afternoon, she overhears a snippet of conversation between two of her team members, Lacy and Len, discussing the project's progress. From what little she catches, Sheila reads too much into it, inferring that they are dissatisfied with her leadership and believe the project is headed for failure. Instead of seeking the truth, Sheila's mind is filled with negative thoughts. She begins to think that her team doesn't trust her judgment and worries that they might be conspiring to

Learning to Catch, Confront, and Change negative self-talk builds confidence.

share their concerns with her manager. The Mind Reader Monster leads her to emotionally withdraw from her team and begin micromanaging every aspect of the project.

How can Sheila's Maverick help reframe this situation?

Catch It: _____

_____

Confront It: _____

_____

Change It: _____

_____

Monster Archetype 4: The Overgeneralizer

Like the Mind Reader, the Overgeneralizer is skilled at blowing up one piece of information into an entire opera. People who overgeneralize use words like *always*, *never*, *everyone*, and *nobody*. For example, "I never do anything right" or "Everyone is always against me in team meetings." This distortion makes people blind to evidence that contradicts the generalization. For instance, even when someone has succeeded in many areas, they focus on their one recent failure. Too often, this becomes a self-fulfilling prophecy. If your Overgeneralizer Monster tells you "You always fail," chances are good that you'll avoid challenges, thereby limiting your opportunities for future success. And when people feel trapped by broad, negative perceptions, they can become susceptible to feelings of frustration, hopelessness, and depression.

How can these Overgeneralizer Monsters be tamed?

Overgeneralizer Headamental #1

After giving a presentation that received rave reviews, Ari posts about it on LinkedIn. While many of his colleagues added celebratory comments or liked his post, Ari can't stop thinking about his boss's unemotional "Thanks." It's running on an endless loop in his brain, and he can't get rid of it, no matter how hard he tries. Days after the presentation, Ari still acts as if that one-word remark characterizes how his audience of 157 responded to his pitch. Before long, he's thinking "I'm always bad at everything. I'll never be a good speaker." This causes him to avoid future speaking opportunities, reinforcing his fear and preventing him from improving his skills.

How can Ari's Maverick help reframe this situation?

Catch It: _____

_____

Confront It: _____

_____

Change It: _____

_____

Overgeneralizer Headamental #2

Zara is a new executive at a tech start-up. She recently gave a presentation to a group of potential investors, showcasing the company's latest product. The presentation went well, and most of the investors seemed enthusiastic and impressed. However, during the Q&A session, one investor made a harsh comment, suggesting that the product's design could be better. Despite receiving numerous positive remarks and expressions of interest, Zara can't help but shake the one negative comment. She starts to believe that if one investor thinks the design is outdated, then the entire product is likely flawed. *Will all potential customers and investors think the same?* This thought process leaves her crippled as her Monster easily convinces Zara to doubt the product's viability and minimize the team's hard work. Behaving like an Overgeneralizer causes her to lose confidence in the product. She even goes so far as to think about killing the product, and her doubts start to affect the rest of the team.

How can Zara's Maverick help reframe this situation?

Catch It:

Confront It:

Change It:

Monster Archetype #5: The Should-er

The cognitive distortion of a Should-er imposes rigid expectations about what they or someone else *should* do. Characterized by using words like *should*, *must*, or *have to*, a Should-er's unrealistic, perfectionistic standards don't acknowledge the complexities of life. These statements set up unrealistic or excessive demands, often resulting in unnecessary pressure. When people don't behave the way a Should-er thinks they should, they respond with frustration, guilt, or resentment. A Should-er approach can also interfere with constructive problem-solving because it focuses on how things *should* be rather than on what can realistically be done to improve a situation.

Here are two Should-er Headamentals. Help them to overcome their Monster.

Should-er Headamental #1

Jenna, a project manager, believes she should always meet her deadlines without fail. When a key supplier delays a shipment, Jenna blames herself, thinking, "I should have anticipated this!" Despite having done everything within her control, she feels guilty and anxious, convinced that she has dropped the ball. This stress prevents her from focusing on finding a solution and collaborating effectively with her team. Jenna's rigid belief that she *should* have seen this coming leads to unnecessary self-criticism ("I'm a failure") and disrupts her ability to manage the situation with a calm, problem-solving mindset.

How can Jenna's Maverick help reframe this situation?

Catch It: _____

_____

Confront It: _____

_____

Change It: _____

_____

Should-er Headamental #2

Raj, a new employee, believes he should quickly master all aspects of his job without needing to ask for help. When he struggles to figure out how to do something he's never done before, he hesitates to ask his colleagues for assistance, thinking, "I should know this by now!" This belief makes him feel inadequate and isolated, and he loses a lot of time trying to solve the problem on his own. Raj's fear of appearing incompetent prevents him from utilizing the support and resources available to him, ultimately slowing down his learning process.

How can Raj's Maverick help reframe this situation?

Catch It: _____

_____

Confront It: _____

_____

Change It: _____

_____

What did you discover by running the above Headamentals? Did you see yourself in one or more of the above Monster Archetypes? How about one of your coworkers? What did you learn about yourself? Which of the Big 5 spotlighted in CAMOS might your Monster be manifesting? Is it wreaking havoc in your mind or for your team?

> **MAVERICK PRO TIP**
>
> Schedule a "CAMOS Audit" on your calendar. Repeat this monthly to consider if you are exhibiting any of these Monster Archetype behaviors. Frequent self-analysis and scheduled awareness time will help you shift from theory to practice.

If you took the time to apply the 3-C Maverick Method to each of these five dominant cognitive distortions and their related Headamentals, you should now have a clearer picture of the system's effectiveness. It's easy to identify how others should behave, respond, or react to a given situation. It's not so easy to identify the same in ourselves.

When we learn to Catch, Confront, and Change negative self-talk, we are practicing the fine art of training our Monster to stand down and move to the back seat of our brains. The very act of practicing—as any burgeoning piano prodigy will tell you—builds confidence, brings you closer to your goals, and enhances proficiency in any given endeavor.

13

Mastering Maverick Habits through Action

Stop worrying about what can go wrong and get excited about what can go right.

TONY ROBBINS

IT'S TIME, now, to officially transfer the decision-making power from your Monster to your Maverick. While it would be nice to pass that behavioral baton by merely flipping a switch, research indicates it takes sixty-six days on average for a new behavior to become a habit. Of course, the length of time it takes to build a new habit or remove a negative one varies widely depending on the individual and the behavior.

Deciding to replace damaging and negative automatic behaviors and thoughts with behaviors and thoughts that support a healthier, more value-aligned, productive life is the final step in the process of change. It's what will enable you to prevent your Monster from ruling your inner world and put your Maverick squarely in the driver's seat.

Pinterest's VP of creative Xanthe Wells says, "I don't experience a lot of negative self-talk. And when I do, I ignore it/set it aside and focus on productivity. The only thing I can control is the amount of effort I put into something that exists in the real world. Delivering consistently good work is the surest way to combat self-doubt because it's tangible proof of why one should be self-confident, not self-doubting. And if you deliver enough of that kind of thing over time, you have a lot to look back on to be proud of." We love how Xanthe uses her Maverick to act and focus on productivity.

Consciously "flipping the switch" from Monster to Maverick is the spark that ignites your replacement behavior. You can't change your current narratives if you don't choose new ones that serve you. The choice must be yours.

Once you choose to change the negative internal narratives that drain your energy and time, you give yourself permission to engage in more productive, nourishing actions and conversations. And as you now know, negative narratives don't start with you. Specific experiences and individuals in your past set that ball in motion. But you're what keeps them playing on repeat. When you create a replacement thought or belief, you rewrite a truer and more empowering understanding of yourself.

Please note that this practice requires total and often brutal honesty and commitment, but luckily, your Maverick always tells the truth, no matter how tough it is. Undoubtedly, you'll find yourself replaying harmful narratives again and again until you master this practice, but with tools at the ready, you can switch out old habits for better alternatives that energize and encourage you.

The Buddhist parable of the second arrow offers guidance on how to deal with unexpected challenges and setbacks.

Imagine you're walking through the woods when suddenly you're struck by an arrow. The pain of the arrow piercing your flesh is intense, and you cry out in agony. However, instead of dealing with the wound and seeking medical attention, you're consumed with anger and resentment toward whoever shot you.

You also obsess over the questions Why me? Why was I the one shot? *You might spend hours or even days stewing over the injustice of the situation while neglecting your own physical and emotional needs. This is the second arrow, a self-inflicted wound that's filled with destructive inner dialogue.*

One of the most important concepts to grasp is the difference between things within your control and things beyond your control, and it's a hard lesson to master. Unless you learn to Catch, Confront, and Change that dialogue, the second arrow will land almost immediately after the first one.

Stephen Gaonach has spent a career navigating corporate America, including the behemoth task of running beloved brand Heinz. For all the love Heinz ketchup has brought to buns across the globe, and with the daunting task of growing the brand well into the future, there were certainly moments where love was the furthest thing from Steve's mind. In other words, stress, anxiety, and overthinking can slow Steve and his team down to the very same pace it takes for Heinz ketchup to leave the bottle! When he is acting as his own worst enemy, Steve acknowledges: "My best antidote is to stop thinking and start doing. I've generally found that if I can just start the thing I am worried about, and I can find even a glimmer of proof positive that it is working, then I am usually OK."

You'll no doubt face challenges in your life when you have very little control over what happens to you. And you can't control other people's behavior, beliefs, or decisions, national and global policies, the weather, and myriad other maddening events. But, as Steve suggests, often it's "less think" and "more do" that gets us through. It's focusing on controlling the controllables. Simply stated, taking action starts with you.

Once you accept the uncontrollable aspects of your life, you can redirect your energy toward the areas where you can make a positive difference. The well-known Serenity Prayer, written by American theologian and pastor Reinhold Niebuhr, captures this important lesson well:

"Grant me the serenity to accept the things I cannot change, the courage to change the things I can, and the wisdom to know the difference."

When it comes to taking action, there are several important elements that are within our control. Specifically, we can control our behavior, our emotions (at least on a good day), and how we react to things (the second arrow). Instead of dwelling on negative emotions, choose to focus on what you can control and do what's necessary to heal and move forward.

Headamentals: The 3-Cs to Switch into Action

The 3-C Maverick Method is a "switch-into-action" plan that invites you to jot down some ideas about the state you're in, why you're in it, and how you can replace your Monster with your Maverick to set yourself up for success. This visualization exercise is a "stop and smell the roses" moment. This plan's simple inquiry process teases apart your derailing thoughts so you can choose a new positive narrative.

Why is a plan necessary? The answer is simple: Intentionality feeds our reality. Habits rule our lives. We don't have enough active brain power to consciously think about everything we're doing every minute of the day. Similarly, if we constantly use willpower to force positive thoughts into our lives, we'll quickly burn out. By developing the intentional habit of switching to positive narratives, it becomes a default setting as opposed to a daily struggle. In physics, the concept of entropy represents a state of chaos, randomness, and disorder. And if you don't focus on your inner narratives, they too will collapse into spiraling chaos.

Choose three negative thoughts you encounter frequently and run them through the 3-C Maverick Method.

Developing the intentional habit of switching to positive narratives becomes a default setting as opposed to a daily struggle.

> **MAVERICK PRO TIP**
>
> Do you do your best thinking when you wake up fresh? Or are you a night owl who prefers total silence? Attack this exercise at your optimal thinking time. You know you best.

Old Narrative 1: Catch It

I can't _____

Because _____

_____

My current Monster Archetype is _____

My Monster is holding me back by _____

_____

_____

New Narrative 1: Confront It

I know my old narrative isn't accurate because _____

_____

_____

Here's what *is* true:
_____
_____
_____
_____

New Behavior 1: Change It
Now that I'm clear about things, here's what I'm going to do:
_____
_____
_____

Old Narrative 2: Catch It

I can't _____

Because _____

_____

My current Monster Archetype is

_____

My Monster is holding me back by

_____
_____
_____

New Narrative 2: Confront It

I know my old narrative isn't accurate because

_____
_____
_____

Here's what *is* true:

_____
_____
_____

New Behavior 2: Change It

Now that I'm clear about things, here's what I'm going to do:

_____
_____
_____

Old Narrative 3: Catch It

I can't _____

Because _____

_____

My current Monster Archetype is

_____

My Monster is holding me back by

_____
_____
_____

New Narrative 3: Confront It

I know my old narrative isn't accurate because

_____
_____

Here's what *is* true:

_____
_____
_____
_____

New Behavior 3: Change It

Now that I'm clear about things, here's what I'm going to do:

_____
_____
_____

What did you learn about yourself?

_____
_____
_____

The goal here is to ensure your brain has developed the habit of identifying which Monster Archetype is at play and running its negative ruminations through the 3-Cs.

Additionally, what aspects of the situations you described can you control, and what can't you control? Focusing energy on things within your command fosters agency and boosts confidence in your ability to solve problems, overcome challenges, and pursue your goals with a clear sense of possibility. It also instills a sense of calm and resilience.

Automatic Maverick

Certain daily activities are automatic and don't require too much brain power: brushing your teeth, folding laundry, driving to work, unloading the dishwasher, taking a shower… The goal is for positive Maverick thoughts to become just as automatic. Think of it as a default trigger toward the positive.

Most people start this process from a defensive position; they're busy fighting off negativity. But instead of fighting "bad" thoughts, think about how you can use them.

Rhett has a coaching client who is a successful but hotheaded entrepreneur. He overreacts whenever life throws him a curveball, which has damaged his relationships with clients and his team. Rhett had his client start small. He asked him to put twenty dollars in a jar every time he lost his temper. The money would be donated to a local charity of his team's choice. His outbursts have decreased in frequency and intensity. The action of paying a fine reminds him to stop and fix his behavior in the moment.

Over time, Rhett's client was ready for a larger behavioral commitment, which included a meditation practice to work on his anger problem.

When you catch yourself thinking "I suck" or "I'm so bad at this" or any number of unhelpful thoughts, flip the switch and say to yourself, "Thanks, Maverick, for reminding me that, over time, I can flip the switch on this. It's time to visualize myself making progress. Brain switch, *go!*"

This creates an "always-win" mechanism: either your Monster becomes disgusted and leaves you alone, or its nagging will inspire you to create and maintain a host of Maverick-inspired positive habits to counterbalance the self-doubt. Either way, it will be a proactive pendulum that swings your negative story to positive encouragement.

The Quest of the Questions

Earlier in the book, we talked about the importance of asking the right questions. Marshall Goldsmith, considered the number one executive coach in the world by many, is a master of this practice. If you follow Marshall, then you're aware of his Daily Questions. This intentional process is a powerful tool for improving personal and professional effectiveness. It involves asking yourself a set of questions every day to measure your effort in doing what matters to you.

According to Marshall, humans are superior planners and inferior doers. Marshall shares, "Daily Questions is a tool I picked up fifteen years ago to deal with my repeating pattern of well-meaning intention followed by unreliable execution."

You know when the number one executive coach on the planet must create a daily practice to keep himself on track, we'd be wise to follow suit.

Headamentals: Goldsmith's Daily Questions

Below are a few ritual questions you might consider asking yourself about your Monster. And, if you can't carve out space daily, consider doing it weekly.

1. Did I do my best to spot a time in the day when my Monster showed up?
2. Did I do my best to understand a behavior or pattern that triggers my Monster?
3. Did I do my best to call on my Maverick to provide a good substitute for the negativity my Monster is feeding me?
4. Did I do my best to identify one or more of the CAMOS?
5. Did I do my best to audit each of the 3-Cs—Catch It, Confront It, Change It—as it pertains to squelching the Monster du jour?

You'll notice that these questions all begin with, "Did I do my best to..." The questions are intended to be answered on a scale from 1 to 10, with 1 indicating "not at all" and 10 indicating "completely."

Some people choose to record their daily responses to the questions on a spreadsheet and identify areas where they can improve their performance the next day. Others use a simple Yes/No response to their Daily Questions. Choose the approach that's best for you.

Unlike traditional methods that focus solely on outcomes, this approach measures the effort you put in, rather than just the results. It fosters a sense of personal ownership and responsibility. Along the way, there's room for both progress and, hopefully, grace—acknowledging that some days will be easier than others. By regularly reflecting on these questions and turning this into a ritual, your Maverick gains another tool to manage your Monster.

The Accountability Piece

If you want to increase the likelihood that Daily Questions will truly make a difference in your life, enlist an accountability partner to serve as your Catch It buddy, someone with whom you can share your Daily Questions and answers each day.

Suzy's accountability partner, John, calls her every day at 8 a.m., and they talk about how well they are living into the things that really matter to them. Rhett and his accountability partner hold a five-minute check-in call at the end of each day to briefly review how far they have progressed with their goals for the day and discuss what they'd like to accomplish the following day.

Starting a conversation with an accountability friend can be awkward, so here's a script to help you get started:

Hey, I'm reading this book called Headamentals: How Leaders Can Crack Negative Self-Talk. *I've realized how much my internal negativity is holding me back. Does that ever happen to you? Do you want to work on this together? I have a few ideas…*

Partnering with a friend or colleague helps you stay focused and positive because few of us have the discipline, courage, and motivation to change our habits without some support. Remember, your Monster would love nothing more than unfettered access to your mind at all times. The sooner you make it a two-on-one by bringing an accountability partner into the fold, the sooner you will learn to silence the Monster.

Research conducted by the Institute for Training and Development on the value of a simple support system is compelling:

- People have a 25 percent probability of success once they have a clear intention to achieve a goal.
- This increases to a 50 percent probability of success if they set a finite time frame and a plan for achieving the goal.

- And their probability of success rockets to 95 percent if they regularly share their progress with a designated person or team.

Building better mental Maverick habits, alone or with an accountability partner, probably sounds like a tall order at first. We've been there. Making the conscious, intentional decision to adopt new behaviors and attitudes can feel like deciding to climb Mount Everest in a pair of sneakers. Our goal is to provide you with the proper equipment to make the successful climb up your Mental Mountain. By understanding how the Big 5 Monster Archetypes worm their way into your brain and learning to dismantle their ridiculousness with the 3-C Maverick Method, you've combined process with practice and are well on your way up the productivity peak.

Want even more ideas to help you outsmart the Big 5 Monster Archetypes? These resources will help you recognize their tricks—and take back control.

CHECK YOURSELF CHECKPOINT

Now we're cooking with gas! In Part Three, we put the father of cognitive therapy Aaron Beck's cognitive distortions under a microscope and magnified the Big 5 Monster Archetypes, aka CAMOS. You took action by reframing the negative Monster narratives to Maverick winning strategies. You learned how to retrain your brain by proactively developing new skills such as the 3-C Maverick Method, the quest of the questions, and the creation of an accountability Catch It buddy.

Before we move on to Part Four, take a quick moment to check yourself using the following five prompts. Remember, none of your answers is final or fatal. This is simply a quick opportunity to touch base with yourself:

Which of the CAMOS is your largest "watch out"?

___

Why do you believe you chose that Monster Archetype?

___

___

Using the 3-C Maverick Method, how might you Catch, Confront, and Change It in the future?

___

___

___

List one person at work who would make a good Catch It buddy.

___

List one person in your personal life who would make a good Catch It buddy.

___

While you've done the excellent and necessary work of getting yourself through the maze of Monster narratives, the hardest work still lies ahead, especially if you are a leader of people. Just like you, everyone on your team is dealing with their own Monster. Now is the time to take what you've learned about yourself and pay it forward. Team-talk is a direct extension of a leader's self-talk, so if you want your team to function at its highest level of productivity and harmony (and who doesn't want that?), you're in the right place.

PART FOUR

The Plutonium
Team-Talk

14

Team-Talk Starts at the Top

In teamwork, silence isn't golden, it's deadly.

MARK SANBORN

HERE WE ARE. You have now reached the summit of your very own Mental Mountain. While we've played the trusted role of Mind Sherpas, you're the one who has done the important work of collecting the necessary tools to conquer your own self-talk.

Like most climbers who commit to the hard task of ascending a high peak, it's difficult to see beyond what's right in front of you. Only when they arrive at the summit do most mountaineers discover, before their very eyes, an even larger mountain waiting for them.

While you've devoted the time and energy to ensure you don't lose yourself, or lose *to* yourself, along the way, it's important to remember that you're not the only one navigating a Monster.

Let's call this book what it is—a business book about leading. If you picked up *Headamentals*, you're already a leader, or you intend to lead one day. If you're already leading, people are following, which requires building real relationships that go beyond the standard, surface-level question "How was your weekend?" Real relationships start by meeting people where they are, which means being attuned to what they're going through and the mental hurdles they face.

> **MAVERICK PRO TIP**
>
> Make *Headamentals* a mandatory read for your team. Create space in meetings to discuss people's Monsters. Take this private matter and make it public across your team.

Picture this: It's Monday morning. You're jumping into your first virtual team meeting of the day. As you look around the Zoom, you notice there are eleven other coworkers on the call, each one listening intently to your project manager. Glance at the person in the box to the left of you. Now, look at the person on your right. Just like you, each has a Monster in their mind who, to varying degrees, is gabbing in their ear. Everyone's dealing with their own inner challenges—impostor syndrome, self-handicapping, confirmation bias, experiential avoidance, amygdala hijacks, and overthinking. You can pretty much guarantee that each of them will have a slightly different interpretation of what the project manager says.

As the leader of this team, are you worrying about your own thoughts, or are you considering how each of your teammates is going fifteen rounds with their Monster? Noticing how, when, and why self-talk impacts individual team members provides key data points that often go undetected. A critical force differentiator leadership skill is to recognize and acknowledge that everyone is dealing with negative self-talk, which can quickly escalate to debilitating team-talk and smash innovation, new initiatives, and fresh ideas like King Kong on a city-wide bender.

One of the best weapons for defanging the Monster in your team members' minds is instilling healthy team-talk behaviors and practices. Your job as a leader is to bring this topic to the forefront. It's the elephant in the room, and a courageous conversation can make all the difference between success and failure.

What is a leader if not a human who can thoughtfully jump into the shoes—and loud minds—of the people they strive to lead? When negative self-talk wins with even just one person on your team, the whole team loses. They lose time. They lose clarity. They may even lose faith and confidence. They definitely lose productivity.

Myriad studies have consistently highlighted the power of positive self-talk in improving team performance. And interventions focused on promoting positive self-talk have also been linked to greater employee engagement, job satisfaction, and overall productivity. In addition, executives who incorporate positive self-talk into their weekly routines demonstrate enhanced resilience when confronted with challenges.

The Practice of Self-Leadership

Before we launch into effective leadership practices to bolster team-talk, we need to point out a Captain Obvious observation: All leadership starts with self-leadership. Self-leadership is a prerequisite for leading anyone else. You wouldn't ask others to walk in arenas you haven't walked yourself, correct? So, let's get to it.

The path to self-leadership starts with self-awareness, and no one is better at bullying yourself than you are. By now, you've most certainly given some thought to where your negative narratives come from. Maybe you've realized what's true and what's not true for you.

Let's take a minute to talk about what self-leadership is and why it matters. Self-leadership is the practice of understanding who you are, what your goals are, and intentionally

Self-leadership starts with self-awareness but culminates in self-love.

making progress toward achieving them. It's about taking charge of your choices, gaining the resilience to face setbacks without losing heart, and successfully adapting to changing circumstances.

People who excel at self-leadership have three things in common:

1. Clear goals for their personal and professional lives.
2. Energy and enthusiasm for learning and growing.
3. The focus and discipline to develop and execute on thoughtful plans and realistic timelines that will enable them to achieve their goals.

People who practice self-leadership feel a clear sense of ownership and empowerment. They are accountable for their decisions and the results they achieve. Psychologist Albert Bandura first wrote about self-leadership in 1977. He named the concept "self-efficacy." Also known as agency, it's the sense of control people feel over their actions and the resulting consequences. More specifically, agency is a person's ability to exert power, make decisions, and take actions that influence their life and circumstances. Many of the things we've talked about—impostor syndrome, self-handicapping, confirmation bias, experiential avoidance, amygdala hijacks, and overthinking—can negatively impact your ability to feel the sense of agency that is essential to practicing self-leadership.

Here's one more truth about self-leadership: in most cases, self-leadership starts with self-awareness but culminates in self-love. Now, before you roll your eyes, don't panic. We're not going to ask you to join a kumbaya circle. We simply want you to be aware that people follow people. And leaders who know themselves well enough to acknowledge their own imperfections are the type of leaders people, lovingly, want to follow.

Sheryl Sandberg is this type of leader. As most of you might remember, she served as the chief operating officer of Facebook (now Meta) for fourteen years and is widely credited with shaping the company's monetization strategy. Sandberg nudges leaders to embrace their freckles, acknowledge their flaws, and laugh at their imperfections, which demonstrates self-awareness and humility while fostering approachability and trust. Sandberg has said on the topic, "We cannot change what we are not aware of, and once we are aware, we cannot help but change." That sounds like a leader who has agency. Sandberg is self-aware and practices self-love.

Headamentals: Self-Leadership Score

Let's take a quick temperature check of your own self-leadership skills. Here's an assessment to understand the extent to which you have agency in your life. It's a short list of statements that may or may not describe you and your reactions to situations. Please consider the extent to which you agree or disagree with each statement and assign each response the appropriate numerical value:

Strongly Disagree: 1
Disagree: 2
Neither Agree nor Disagree: 3
Agree: 4
Strongly Agree: 5

Set aside ten minutes to complete this assessment in a quiet place. For the most accurate results, choose the first answer that comes to mind—and be honest.

1. I feel in control of my decisions and actions. _____

2. When faced with a challenge, I work hard to influence the outcome. _____

3. I take responsibility for the consequences of my decisions. _____

4. When I set my mind to something, I work hard to make it happen. _____

5. When things don't go as planned, I look for ways to adapt or improve the situation. _____

6. I'm comfortable making important decisions without relying solely on others' opinions. _____

7. I view obstacles as challenges to be overcome rather than insurmountable barriers. _____

8. I actively seek out information and resources to help me achieve my objectives. _____

9. I believe I have the power to create positive change in my life. _____

10. When I make a mistake, I see it as an opportunity to learn and grow. _____

11. I feel confident in my ability to handle unexpected situations. _____

12 I actively voice my opinions and ideas, even if they differ from those of others. _____

13 I take initiative in solving problems rather than waiting for others to fix them. _____

14 If I put my mind to it, I'm able to break a bad habit. _____

15 I seek the resources I need to help me achieve my objectives. _____

TOTAL _____

To score this assessment, add up the ratings for all items. The total score will range from 15 to 75 points.

53–75 points: Strong self-leadership. You believe in your own capabilities. You take control of situations, confident that your decisions and actions make a real difference. When challenges arise, you see them as opportunities to learn and grow rather than as threats to your competence. Even setbacks are met with resilience as you understand that each experience contributes to your overall journey. You celebrate your successes, learn from your mistakes, and consistently empower yourself to take on new challenges, fully trusting in your ability to navigate whatever comes your way.

31–52 points: Moderate self-leadership. You usually trust your abilities and take initiative, but you also recognize that there are times when you could benefit from a second opinion or a little extra preparation. You typically feel capable of handling challenges on your own, yet an occasional hint of uncertainty nudges you to pause and gather more information. This balanced approach lets you act decisively, most of the time, while remaining open to learning and collaboration when needed.

15–30 points: Minimal self-leadership. You often feel that your actions have little impact on the outcome of events. When challenges arise, you hesitate to step forward because you doubt that your efforts will truly make a difference. Instead of trusting your own instincts, you tend to wait for guidance or rely on others to lead the way. This lingering uncertainty leaves you feeling somewhat detached, as if circumstances around you dictate your path more than any decisions you make.

Minimize the Noise

If you feel like you're not in control of your team (or your life), one of the most effective ways to increase your sense of agency is by controlling the stimuli in your environment. We know it's easier said than done, but when you're able to manage your surroundings you're better able to focus your attention and feel more in control. If you can implement any of the following suggestions, you'll be ahead of the game:

- Create quiet, screen-free spaces to escape overstimulation.
- Turn off your phone notifications while working.
- Spend time in nature.
- Avoid noisy or distracting environments.

The CliffsNotes version: remove what's unnecessary from your mind so you can focus on what matters most. Realistically, we can't handle much more than that anyway. So, let's do what we can to keep the main thing the main thing.

We are a distracted species. And we're less skilled at multitasking than we think.

To showcase just how "at capacity" humans are, we turn to a well-known and often cited psychology study by researcher George Miller, who makes the point that we should all should strive to be master minimizers. In this study, Miller discovered that people can only juggle seven "chunks" of information (plus or minus two) at any given time. Anything above that, and we begin to overwhelm and exhaust ourselves.

When you feel cloudy, confused, and out of control, consider taking a page from famed hostage negotiator Chris Voss. The author of *Never Split the Difference: Negotiating as if Your Life Depended on It*, Chris has experienced some of the highest-pressure scenarios imaginable. From bank robbers to Harlem shoot-outs, the FBI has relied on Chris to calmly restore balance while bringing both hostages and bad guys in unharmed. He's the first to admit, "After two decades negotiating for human lives, you still feel fear."

Chris goes into detail about what it was like entering into the hijack and hostage business early in his life. To stay successful in this unconventional space and be able to hijack the mind of a hijacker, Chris had to develop a critical skill. It starts with turning off his own assumptions about what the hijacker wants. Instead, he learned to quiet both his Monster and his Maverick, so he can focus all his energy on understanding the motivations of the person he's negotiating with.

Chris says, "It may look like there are only two people in a conversation, but really it's more like four people talking all at once." He openly acknowledges the realness of both parties' self-talk during a pressure cooker scenario.

You are most likely going through a high-stakes project right now with your team. This endless tension has upped the anxiety across your direct reports. You are the leader, and you want to convey strength.

We're here to tell you that a strong mind is one that remains an open mind. Sometimes the best trait a leader can unlock is the ability to silence both their Monster and their Maverick. To develop the muscle of active listening and do what Chris Voss does, empathize with the Monster that may live inside the mind of the person across the table. While doing a listening lap may seem contradictory to picking up speed, slowing down long enough to create a psychologically safe space for people to genuinely share what their Monster is cooking up is the fastest way to build trust, cement engagement, and create alignment on a shared goal.

15

Business Is a Team Sport

A group becomes a team when each member is sure enough of themselves and their contributions to praise the skills of others.

NORMAN SHIDLE

IN THE BUSINESS WORLD, performance matters. While many legacy organizations see themselves as a family, the hard truth is we're rarely pink-slipping our uncles, cousins, and siblings. More realistically, our workforces need to function like sports teams do.

Time under Tension

If talent is the gold medal, and team is the silver medal, then time is the bronze. Winning teams know that success is often decided in seconds, not minutes. A perfect example of this is a NASCAR pit crew.

While races may be won on the track, they are also won—and lost—in the pit. Each crew member has one focused task to do in under ten seconds: changing tires, refueling, and making critical mechanical adjustments. The training that goes into perfecting these pit stops is no less rigorous than the drivers' preparation.

Chad Knaus is one of the sport's most successful crew chiefs. As team leader, Knaus led Jimmie Johnson to seven NASCAR Cup Series championships, a feat built on meticulous preparation, novel strategies, and flawless team execution. His success was no accident. He fostered a culture where every member of the team knew their responsibility down to the smallest detail. From the jackman to the tire changers, everyone worked in unison toward a common shared goal: shaving those vital seconds off in the pit. When the talk track of each individual aligned with the team's shared reality, that's when they performed at their best. Knaus's illustrious career culminated in his 2024 induction into the NASCAR Hall of Fame, cementing his legacy as one of the greatest crew chiefs in history.

This same principle Knaus employed applies beyond the track. In sports or in business, when communication is disjointed or unclear, teams slow down. Great teams communicate seamlessly, and when everyone is on the same page with their team-talk, even the most challenging tasks can be executed with precision. Just like a NASCAR pit crew, high-performing teams thrive on the shared understanding that their success relies on each individual performing their role with confidence and efficiency.

Let's acknowledge that if you've reached this point in our book, you have ambitious plans to stay curious across a blossoming career. We're guessing you're the type who likes a meaty project at work; the kind of project not everyone signs up for. You may even like the pressure associated with those types of challenges. Most of the pressure comes from putting yourself in a leadership position, not necessarily by title but by the responsibility you take on. You step up to the plate, or into the pit, to be a critical cog on the team, for the team.

In his first book, Ryan taught us that the sole goal of leadership is "Believership." When working with a team, people either believe in what they are working toward or they are fake believers. Any meaningful project is rarely a solo journey:

it takes a village. In other words, there is no DIY, only DIT. While do-it-yourself flies for those home projects, do-it-together is the only way a challenging project will make it over the finish line in an organization.

Operational Unity

Keeping with the theme that business is a team sport, consider the history-making performance(s) of one of the greatest teams the world of sports has ever witnessed. The Chicago Bulls, under the leadership of Phil Jackson and Michael Jordan, are widely regarded as the best team in NBA history, particularly during their two three-peats in the 1990s. What made this team exceptional wasn't just the talents of the individual players. It was their ability to come together, silence their individual self-talk, and align under one unified shared goal: greatness.

Phil Jackson, the "Zen Master," brought a one-of-a-kind coaching philosophy that transformed the Bulls.

His approach was rooted in a commitment to something bigger than individual accolades. His focus on authenticity and intentionality helped the Bulls develop trust and reliance on one another, forming a cohesive unit that played with one mind.

"I can't pretend to be an expert in leadership theory," Jackson has said. "But what I do know is that the art of transforming a group of young, ambitious individuals into an integrated championship team is not a mechanistic process. It's a mysterious juggling act that requires not only a thorough knowledge of the time-honored laws of the game, but also an open heart, a clear mind, and a deep curiosity about the ways of the human spirit."

At the center of Jackson's coaching style was the "triangle offense," a system that mandated every player selflessly share the ball to contribute to the team's success. "What attracted me to the triangle was the way it empowers the players, offering each one a vital role to play as well as a high level of creativity within a clear, well defined structure... All five players must be fully engaged every second or the whole system will fail. That stimulates an ongoing process of group problem-solving in real time, not just on a coach's clipboard during timeout."

However, the transformation wasn't exactly easy. Michael Jordan, the team's biggest star, initially resisted the triangle offense. Used to relying on his own abilities, Jordan had to shift his mindset from individual dominance to trusting his coach and his teammates. Once Jordan bought into the system, the rest of the team followed, leading to a new level of synchronicity on the court.

Jordan, confirming he is human like the rest of us, admitted to moments when he battled his own self-talk. Beyond the technical aspects of the game, Jackson worked closely with sports psychologist George Mumford, who introduced mindfulness practices to all players. He taught the players to silence their internal self-talk Monster and stay fully present in the moment, which was key to their sustained excellence. In particular, he taught Jordan to remain calm under the intense pressure of the NBA playoffs. Jordan is not shy about crediting Mumford's influence on his game.

The Bulls' mental clarity allowed them to thrive in pivotal situations and maintain a collective focus on their shared goal of greatness. When Jordan embraced Jackson's triangle offense and Mumford's mindfulness strategies for peak performance, his leadership evolved. He was not only a scoring machine, but also a teammate who trusted the system and

Positive team-talk is characterized by open, affirming, and supportive communication.

his fellow players. This cultural shift empowered other key players, like Scottie Pippen and Dennis Rodman, to elevate their roles, knowing that the team's success depended on the synergy they created together.

The Bulls' ability to silence their self-talk and align under one clear, operationalized vision of greatness was the foundation of their dynasty. Every player knew their role, trusted the system, and contributed to the team's overarching goal. By matching their mental game with physical execution, they became one of the most successful and unified teams in the history of sports.

The Bulls' journey demonstrates the effectiveness of collective, shared team-talk and its power to drive results.

Effective Communication 101

Team-talk refers to any communication within a team, including verbal, digital, and nonverbal interactions. It is reflected in the team's collective mindset, how they set goals, and approach challenges. Team-talk works a lot like the tide in the ocean; it can either lift all boats or ground the ship.

Positive team-talk is characterized by open, affirming, and supportive communication that fosters a collaborative and resilient environment. This isn't about back slaps and high fives. As a leader, you're not required to play the role of *Saturday Night Live*'s fictional self-help guru Stuart Smalley, who gazed into a mirror and said, "I'm good enough, I'm smart enough, and doggone it, people like me." It's also not your job to transform yourself into Tony Robbins, who only spouts positive affirmations.

Sometimes, a leader's job requires tough love, by which we mean fostering responsibility and self-discipline by setting firm boundaries with the goal of helping every person on the team grow and succeed. This type of leadership plays a crucial role in molding team dynamics and building a culture of trust and mutual respect. When team members believe in their ability to succeed, they are more likely to exert the effort needed to achieve their goals.

> **MAVERICK PRO TIP**
>
> Tough love doesn't mean being a jerk. It means setting clear expectations, and making sure everyone understands how their role contributes to the big picture.

Positive team-talk initiates a virtuous cycle that helps team members believe they can succeed, while negative team-talk triggers a vicious cycle of self-doubt where people throw in the towel rather than rise to the challenge.

Leaders do more than articulate goals and motivate their employees to achieve them. They're also key in helping people summon their Mavericks to keep the mindset needed to tackle and master difficult situations.

Many of the world's most successful companies recognize the importance of team-talk and have incorporated practices to enhance it into their corporate cultures. For example, Microsoft strongly encourages the use of positive self-talk as part of its broader focus on employee well-being and productivity. They share techniques for focusing on constructive and affirming thoughts with their employees. This growth mindset is also reflected in leadership communications, team meetings, and performance reviews. They use their Teams and Viva applications to disseminate resources through regular reminders, tips, and encouragement to fuel their employees' inner Mavericks.

Vicious to Virtuous

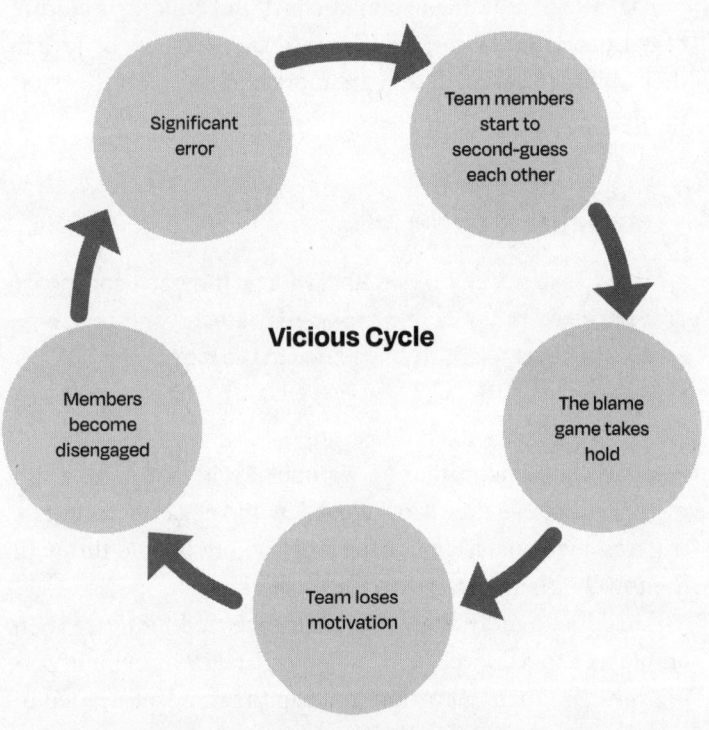

Errors are blown out of proportion and affect team productivity

SpartanNash, a Fortune 500 company, operates as a food distributor and grocery retailer, serving independent and corporate-owned stores, military commissaries, and food service customers across the United States. Ryan's client Nicole Zube is chief HR officer there, responsible for providing the talk track that permeates the brains of over 140 HR employees. One of the ways Ryan helped Nicole develop and maintain that positive talk track is by creating

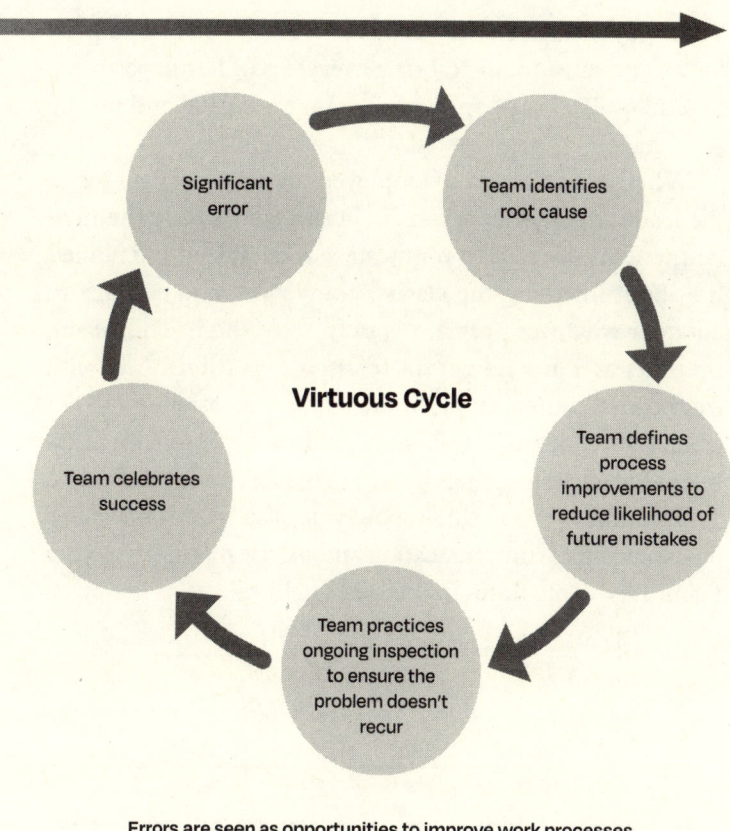

Errors are seen as opportunities to improve work processes

"The Firstie Awards," which are distributed quarterly. The Firsties are given to those on Nicole's team who embody a "people first" mentality, which is the number one core behavior at the company.

Nicole's commitment to supporting both the personal and professional lives of the company's employees is key to its overall success. She is constantly looking for ways to ritualize her team-talk, which includes monthly lunch and learns, a monthly newsletter, and team town halls. She also budgets for an annual summit to bring everyone in her department together "live" to keep the full team energized and on the same page.

Whether you have 140 employees or four, it is your job as the leader to monitor and model team-talk. Create the mentality and mettle to help your team stay energized and unified. It's about injecting the clarity, conviction, and courage to conquer whatever problem is in front of them. This forum presents as a green light for freer conversations. And with freer conversations comes more experimentation, more collaboration, and, most of all, more productivity. More so, a new team characteristic brings its face to the forefront: confidence.

Take some time to think about your plan to encourage and enable positive communication among the members of your team. Take some notes in the space below.

_____

_____

_____

_____

Dog-ear this page, and over the next week, reflect on your ideas. Run them by people on your team. When you think you've properly vetted things, try them out!

Competence Equals Confidence

In the 1950s, emergency medical care was revolutionized with the development of cardiopulmonary resuscitation, best known by most of us as CPR. This work laid the foundation for modern resuscitation techniques, including the advanced cardiac life support (ACLS) protocols that are used today. Despite advancements in ACLS, the chances of surviving a cardiac arrest with full brain function remained wildly low at 8 percent, even with the best medical care. This is where Dr. Joe Bellezzo and his pioneering team enter our story.

Bellezzo, a physician leader in the department of emergency medicine at Sharp Memorial Hospital in San Diego, California, along with his team, had developed a new technique called ECPR (extracorporeal cardiopulmonary resuscitation) which has been shown to increase survival rates by up to five times compared to traditional CPR. This breakthrough represented a major leap forward in its ability to save lives and improve outcomes for patients who experience cardiac arrest.

Of course, in the early days, Bellezzo and his team didn't have proof—they merely had belief. And, over time, when they started to see success with ECPR, a new attribute showed itself across the team: confidence.

Bellezzo recalls, "The whole team now believes in this because we've accomplished something pretty remarkable, even if just once or twice. If you really believe something can work, its chances of survival are much better than if you don't believe in it."

Many leaders and coaches believe that confidence, more than talent, is the true differentiator between good and great teams. A crucial leadership quality, confidence is not something you are born with; it's a skill that can be developed through practice and experience. Just look at Bellezzo's ER team. While doctors rarely suffer from a confidence glitch, Bellezzo's team committed themselves to the same team-talk: *It's possible. Why not us?*

The introduction of ECPR has significantly improved outcomes for cardiac arrest patients. Emergency department cardiopulmonary bypass is not only a groundbreaking accomplishment and medical marvel, but it should also be a corporate case study in the power of belief. Dr. Bellezzo emphasizes that when a team truly believes in their mission, their chances of success skyrocket. His team's belief was the fuel that propelled them to achieve what many thought impossible.

Team confidence is born out of competence, and competence is gained through a focused effort to master knowledge and skills. By creating an environment of continuous learning, your team is encouraged to gain the expertise that will naturally enhance their abilities to act, even in the face of fear.

Despite what many think, confidence isn't reserved for those who are naturally outgoing or bold. It is available to everyone. Use internal meetings as an opportunity to encourage people to talk about their strengths and how they can leverage them. This is a wonderful morale-building activity that helps team members understand more about what each person brings to the table. Asking people to focus on what they do well and finding ways to incorporate their strengths into their team's efforts creates a positive feedback loop.

The success of Dr. Bellezzo's team highlights a powerful lesson about confidence and its impact on achieving the extraordinary. In essence, the belief in their abilities—a mindset shift—became a self-fulfilling prophecy, driving the team to achieve greater success.

No matter what someone's personality, confidence is essential for your team members' success. It allows them to push past their limits, take on new challenges, and recover from setbacks with greater ease. It empowers them to perform at their best, day in and day out. It's the key to unlocking the full potential of every individual member and achieving exceptional results for the whole team.

Teams that are confident in their collective abilities tend to perform better. Just ask Chad Knaus, Jimmie Johnson, Phil Jackson, and Michael Jordan. Winning is contagious. Once a team gets a win under its belt, they are more likely to want to bring their bats to the plate and take another swing. And then another. Confidence begets more confidence, and the onus of success shifts from you, the leader, to the team itself. When the team wins, it gives life to their inner Mavericks, which means everyone is functioning at a level where they are making better decisions, sharing accountability, executing under pressure, and, above all, believing in themselves as individual contributors and team players.

Spend ten minutes thinking about some of your team's successes in the last few months—big and small. In your next team meeting, talk about the wins you've identified and invite them to add to this list. And make this part of every team meeting at least once a month. You'll be amazed at the boost they get when they acknowledge their Maverick moments.

Want to lead your team even more effectively? These resources are loaded with practical, game-changing strategies and tools you can use right away.

16

Cognitive Distortions within Teams

Coming together is the beginning. Keeping together is progress. Working together is success.

HENRY FORD

REMEMBER CAMOS? Not surprisingly, there are team-level cognitive biases and distortions analogous to the individual cognitive distortions we shared in Chapter 12: "The Big 5 Monster Archetypes." These team-level biases significantly impact organizational effectiveness and decision quality. Recognizing and addressing them is crucial for improving team-talk and, ultimately, team performance.

In the following pages, we'll dig into the four most common team-level distortions that leaders need to be hyper-vigilant about detecting and reversing: groupthink, escalation of commitment, illusion of unanimity, and diffusion of responsibility.

Groupthink: The Silent Saboteur of Smart Decisions

Have you ever been in a meeting where everyone nods along in agreement to a preposterous new idea? You're pretty sure the idea and the collective response to it are a classic case of brainstorming gone awry. Welcome to the world of groupthink, the cognitive kryptonite that turns sharp-minded people into yes-folks. Similar to individual black-and-white thinking, groupthink occurs when a team prioritizes consensus over critical evaluation of alternative ideas.

Social psychologist Irving Janis first spotted this phenomenon in the 1970s. He noticed that smart people in tight-knit groups sometimes made spectacularly bad decisions. Why? Because they are loath to rock the boat, ruffle feathers, risk social extrication, or otherwise deviate from the norm. Groupthink is the office equivalent of peer pressure. It's not about what's right; it's about what's least likely to cause a ripple in still waters. In high-stakes situations, where money and jobs are on the line, groupthink can kick into overdrive. Before you know it, the team's desire to keep-the-peace trumps the need for a reality check.

But here's where it gets really interesting. Groupthink isn't just a behavioral quirk. It's hardwired in our brains. When groupthink takes over, our brain's analytical circuits essentially go on vacation and the areas associated with social conformity light up like a Broadway marquis. It's as if our brains are saying, "Who needs critical thinking when we can have a comfortable moment with consensus?" This neural shift prioritizes fitting in over thinking it through. It's not just peer pressure; it's peer-powered brain rewiring.

Here are a few well-known examples of the dangers of groupthink on the world stage:

Bay of Pigs Blunder: In 1961, President John F. Kennedy's advisors—trapped in an echo chamber—ignored dissent and overestimated the chances of success for the Bay of Pigs invasion on the southern coast of Cuba. The disastrous decision resulted in 114 deaths, 1,189 captures, and one red-faced superpower. Lesson learned: a diversity of perspectives beats an insulated group of nonconfrontational yes-people.

***Challenger*'s Chilling Choice:** NASA's 1986 groupthink gamble exploded on liftoff because managers dismissed engineers' concerns about O-ring seals in cold weather. Pressured to launch, they rationalized the risks based on past successes. The tragic explosion killed all seven crew members, forcing NASA to rocket back to Earth and reassess its decision-making culture and processes.

Wall Street's House of Cards: In 2008, the bigwigs in financial behemoths like Lehman Brothers built sandcastles on reckless subprime mortgage investments. They ignored warnings and assumed housing prices would rise indefinitely. When the housing bubble burst, it triggered Lehman's collapse and took the global economy down with it, illustrating groupthink's potential for financial ruin.

How can you protect your team from becoming a groupthink-dominated echo chamber? The following are a few ideas that any leader can operationalize across their team. Don't feel you need to implement all of them. See which ones makes sense for your team.

Raise awareness. Invite your team to talk about instances when they may have fallen prey to groupthink. Dig into the root causes and discuss what they can do to counteract this natural tendency.

Embrace the outsider. Bring in someone who doesn't have a stake in the group's harmony. They're more likely to ask the uncomfortable questions everyone else is avoiding. Consider people from different departments and outside of your organization. Whenever Ryan's company has a big pitch, they simulate the presentation to a few employees who are not involved. Role-playing the prospect, those employees ask questions and point out blind spots. Fresh eyes and ears can spot issues the creators might have overlooked. Plus, explaining ideas to outsiders reveals gaps in your own thinking.

Assign a rotating devil's advocate. In every meeting, designate someone to play devil's advocate and regularly rotate the assignment. This prevents one person from being seen as a constant naysayer and encourages everyone to think critically. The goal isn't to shoot down ideas: the goal is to put them through a stress test. It's like enlisting the services of a professional party pooper but for the greater good.

Encourage anonymous input. Imagine a world where ideas are judged solely on their merit, not on who proposed them. That's the power of anonymous input. Use digital tools or index cards to click through ideas without names attached. You'll be amazed how often the quietest voices have the best ideas when the fear of judgment is removed.

The purpose of these groupthink-busters is to foster an environment where critical thinking is prioritized and encouraged over harmony. After all, the best decisions often come from constructive disagreement. Combating groupthink is about creating a culture where it's OK to say, "I disagree, and here's why." It's about valuing the voice of dissent as much as a chorus of agreement. Because sometimes, the person who's willing to be the lone voice of reason is the one who unlocks the best idea or saves the organization from making an irreversible error.

Headamentals: Psychological Safety Test

Here's a quick survey to see if your team operates within a psychologically safe environment, which is essential for combating groupthink. It's a short list of statements that describe the environment in which you and your team operate. Please consider the extent to which you agree or disagree with each statement and assign each response the appropriate numerical value:

Strongly Disagree: 1
Disagree: 2
Neither Agree nor Disagree: 3
Agree: 4
Strongly Agree: 5

Set aside ten minutes to complete this assessment in a quiet place. For the most accurate results, choose the first answer that comes to mind—and be honest.

1. I feel comfortable expressing my ideas and opinions, even if they differ from others on the team. _____

2. Team members welcome feedback without becoming defensive. _____

3. It's safe to take calculated risks or try new approaches without fear of negative consequences. _____

4. Mistakes are viewed as learning opportunities rather than reasons for criticism. _____

5   I can ask for help from my team without feeling incompetent.   _____

6   During meetings, everyone has a chance to contribute and be heard.   _____

7   Our team leader encourages open discussion and values diverse perspectives.   _____

8   I feel comfortable challenging the way we do things.   _____

9   Team members respect each other's unique backgrounds, skills, and experiences. _____

10 When conflicts arise, they are addressed quickly, openly, and constructively.   _____

TOTAL   _____

Here's how to interpret your results.

41–50 points: There is a high level of psychological safety on your team. People willingly give and accept help and feedback from each other. Open discussion is a way of life, and everyone participates.

26–40 points: Your team is on the road to psychological safety, but they haven't quite arrived. Some people are more comfortable than others sharing their thoughts and challenging the status quo. Be on the lookout for moments that cause people to go back into their shells and call them out in real time.

10–25 points: Your team is just starting to be more comfortable sharing their opinions and asking for help. Encourage everyone to participate and nip any criticism in the bud.

Now, look for any items where the average response is a three or less. These areas demonstrate aspects of psychological safety that may need attention.

Remember, the goal isn't to create a team of constant critics. It's about fostering an environment where assumptions are regularly challenged and the best ideas emerge through rigorous, respectful debate. By implementing these strategies, you're creating a culture of innovation where the next big breakthrough could come from anyone at any time.

The most successful teams aren't those that always agree. They're the ones that know how to disagree productively and turn potential conflict into creative fuel. So, the next time you're in a meeting where everyone's nodding along, the most valuable contribution you can make is a well-placed, "Wait a minute. What if…?"

Escalation of Commitment

Imagine you're on a road trip, and you realize you've been driving in the wrong direction for hours. Do you keep going, hoping that somehow you'll end up at your destination, or do you turn around and get back on track?

In the world of work, teams often find themselves in a similar predicament. They've invested significant time, money, and effort into a project, only to discover they never find themselves nearing the right off-ramp for an optimal result. Instead of changing course, they double down, and pour more resources into the wrong-way idea. This is the essence of escalation of commitment, analogous to individual sunk cost fallacy.

The goal is to foster an environment where assumptions are challenged and the best ideas emerge.

Escalation of commitment is a well-documented psychological trap first identified by psychologist Barry M. Staw in his 1976 study on investment decisions that can lead even the smartest teams astray. Why do we fall into this trap? Our brains are wired to avoid admitting mistakes and to justify our decisions. Here are some of the stories we tell ourselves:

- We've come too far to give up now.
- Just one more push, and we'll turn the corner.
- Quitting would mean all our hard work was for nothing.

These narratives are often more fiction than fact.

What follows are several examples of organizations that were so blinded by illusions of success they couldn't see the looming reality of failure. Though the warning signs were clearly visible in their metrics, they clung to flawed strategies with an iron grip.

The Concorde Catastrophe: For those too young to remember, the Concorde was a supersonic passenger airliner that cut the time of transatlantic transit in half. It was seen as an icon of luxury air travel and aviation engineering. It's also a cautionary tale of ambition gone awry. Britain and France poured billions into their high-velocity dream, stubbornly clinging to a costly commercial vision and pricing themselves out of the very market they intended to serve. In the end, it's a reminder that the hardest part of flying is knowing when and how to land.

Toshiba's Nuclear Meltdown: Toshiba invested in Westinghouse Electric with the goal of expanding its nuclear power business. Despite spiraling losses and a shifting nuclear landscape after the Fukushima disaster, Toshiba doubled down and continued to invest mightily into a sinking ship. Much like the Concorde, knowing when to cut your losses is as vital as chasing gains.

A Military Quagmire: The Vietnam War is a tragic example of escalation of commitment in military strategy. Despite mounting evidence that the war was unwinnable, four successive US administrations escalated involvement, driven by the weight of previous sacrifices. By the time the US withdrew in 1973, the war had cost over fifty-eight thousand American lives and billions of taxpayer dollars, demonstrating the tragic consequences of committing to a failing course of action.

How can teams avoid the escalation of commitment pitfall? Here are some approaches to consider, and once again, use the one(s) that make the most sense for your team.

Raise awareness. Invite your team to talk about times they've experienced or witnessed an escalation of commitment, either at work or in their personal lives, and what they'd do differently in retrospect.

Set clear evaluation criteria up front. Before embarking on a project, establish specific, measurable benchmarks for success. This provides an objective framework for assessing progress and makes it easier to recognize when it's time to change direction.

Conduct regular, honest reviews. Schedule frequent check-ins to evaluate a project's status. These reviews should be candid discussions where team members feel safe to voice concerns without fear of criticism. It's also helpful to invite colleagues who are *not* invested in the project's success to join these meetings at predetermined milestones.

When things aren't going well, reframe sunk costs. When facing the decision to continue or abandon a project, instead of focusing on what you've already invested, ask yourself, "If we were starting from scratch today, knowing what we know now, would we choose to invest in this project?" This question helps cut through the fog of sunk costs and allows you to see the situation with fresh eyes.

Embrace the pivot. Cultivate a culture that values flexibility and sees changing course as a sign of wisdom, not weakness. Celebrate teams that have the courage to abandon failing projects and redirect resources to more promising ventures.

> **MAVERICK PRO TIP**
>
> The most successful teams are the ones that recognize mistakes quickly and have the courage to change their course.

The Illusion of Unanimity

Imagine a world where silence is mistaken for agreement, and nodding heads hide a sea of doubt. This is the realm of the illusion of unanimity, a cognitive trap that can turn smart groups into collective blunderers. Akin to individual mind-reading, in a group setting, silence is often mistaken for agreement without verifying.

Irving Janis, the social psychologist who coined the term *groupthink*, would recognize this scene all too well, and it's a perfect storm of psychological forces:

- We conform to avoid standing out (conformity pressure).
- We assume others agree when they're probably as uncertain as we are (pluralistic ignorance).
- We bite our tongues to keep the peace and protect our social standing (self-censorship).

- We cherry-pick information that supports the apparent consensus (confirmation bias).
- We overestimate how many others share our views (false consensus effect).

Our brains even get in on the act: fMRI studies show our social cognition centers light up when we fall in line with the group. The result? Another dangerous echo chamber where critical thinking suffocates and diverse perspectives vanish.

If you see similarities between the illusion of unanimity and groupthink, you're right. While groupthink is the overall tendency of a cohesive group to prioritize consensus over critical thinking, the illusion of unanimity is the false perception that everyone in the group agrees, even when private doubts or disagreements exist. By creating a false sense that everyone agrees, it suppresses dissent and reinforces the problematic dynamics at the heart of groupthink.

Here are some tragic examples where the illusion of unanimity has caused some of history's most catastrophic decisions, costing companies and countries untold dollars and endless heartache:

Brexit's Slow-Motion Disaster: In Whitehall, British civil servants (like the UK's ambassador to the European Union) had grave concerns about the complexity of leaving the EU. Unfortunately, optimistic politicians promising an easy transition sidelined the people who had to make it happen. Decision-makers with reservations stayed mum, assuming their colleagues must have solutions they weren't aware of. This false consensus led to unrealistic timelines and expectations. As negotiations progressed, the true challenges emerged, turning what was sold as a simple process into a multiyear political and economic quagmire.

Enron's Disastrous Implosion: Enron's board members—blanketed by impressive financial reports and charmed by charismatic executives—chose to ignore red flags like complex off-books partnerships and opaque accounting practices. Meetings consistently ended with apparent consensus on the company's robust health. In truth, several board members harbored serious doubts, but in a culture where dissent was seen as a lack of sophistication, those in doubt remained silent. The result? A $74 billion bankruptcy that became synonymous with corporate fraud, leaving thousands jobless and retirement funds decimated. Sometimes, the most dangerous lies are the ones we tell ourselves.

Coke's Calamitous Rebrand: It's not just life-or-death situations where the illusion of unanimity rears its ugly head. Remember New Coke? No? Well, it didn't last long. In Coca-Cola's Atlanta headquarters, marketing exec Sergio Zyman championed a new formula, while veteran Ike Herbert had grave misgivings about changing the century-old recipe. In meeting after meeting, Herbert's concerns were drowned out by enthusiasm for "beating Pepsi," and the lack of vocal opposition was mistaken for universal agreement. The launch backfired spectacularly, and it took Coca-Cola just seventy-nine days to revert to the original formula, learning a $34 million lesson in the dangers of assumed consensus. Even in marketing, assuming everyone agrees can lead to a very public face-plant.

These stories aren't just cautionary tales, they're calls to action. They challenge us to create environments where dissent is celebrated and where saying "I'm not sure" is seen as a strength not a weakness. Remember, true unanimity is rare. So, the next time you're in a meeting and everyone's just nodding along, ask yourself: "Is this true agreement, or are we all afraid to rock the boat?" It might be time to screw up your courage and say, "Are we sure about this?" The next great idea, or the next disaster averted, might be hiding in that moment of pause.

Here are a few ways to kick any false illusions of unanimity on your team to the curb:

Raise awareness. Invite your team to talk about times they've experienced or witnessed an illusion of unanimity, either at work or in their personal lives, and encourage them to discuss how they might avoid staying silent next time.

Implement silent brainstorming. Before group discussions, give everyone time to write down their thoughts independently. This technique, sometimes called brainwriting, prevents vocal members from dominating and allows quieter voices to be heard. It's amazing how often the best ideas come from unexpected sources when you level the playing field.

Have second chance meetings. After making a decision, schedule a follow-up meeting a week later. This gives people time to reflect on the decision and voice any concerns. Often, the passage of time allows for clear thinking and will surface doubts that were initially suppressed.

By implementing these strategies, you're proactively getting ahead of the high cost of the illusion of unanimity and you're creating a safe space for people to speak up and share their opinions.

Diffusion of Responsibility

Diffusion of responsibility is a well-documented psychological phenomenon that's as perplexing as it is pervasive. First empirically demonstrated by psychologists John Darley and Bibb Latané, it occurs when a specific deliverable or expectation is not attached to a specific person or department. Team members assume someone else will take the lead, and things fall through the cracks. Also known as the bystander effect, diffusion of responsibility has profound implications for understanding group behavior and decision-making processes.

Picture this: a group of people witness an emergency, yet no one steps in to help. Darley and Latané's groundbreaking experiments showed that the greater the number of people present in an emergency, the less likely any individual is to help, as if responsibility evaporates into thin air when diluted among a crowd. It's as if their brains are saying "Not my job!" They're not bad people; they're simply falling prey to a quirk of human behavior.

Organizational behavior studies demonstrate this effect in the workplace. Individuals look to others for cues on how to behave. When people perceived to be of high status don't act, others follow their lead. This can be demonstrated in several different ways:

Pluralistic ignorance: Misinterpreting others' inaction as a sign that help is not needed.

Social loafing: The larger the teams/group, the less effort an individual will exert.

Workplace innovation stagnation: In corporate settings, when high-ranking executives do not actively promote or engage in innovative practices, lower-level employees are less likely to propose or pursue new ideas.

You've probably all heard the "Everybody, Somebody, Anybody, and Nobody" story. It illustrates the problem of diffusion of responsibility in a simple, memorable way:

There was an important job to be done, and Everybody was sure that Somebody would do it. Anybody could have done it, but Nobody did it. Everybody thought Anybody could do it, but Nobody realized that Everybody hadn't done it. Everybody blamed Somebody when Nobody did what Anybody could have done.

Imagine a world where every disaster could be prevented, every crisis averted, if only someone took responsibility. Sound far-fetched? Think again. Some of history's most infamous catastrophes weren't caused by villains but by good people assuming someone else would step up:

Stanford Prison Experiment: In 1971, what started as a simulation turned into a real-life horror show. Why? Because each "guard" thought, "Surely, someone else will stop this if it goes too far." Spoiler alert: No one did. It's a chilling reminder that in groups, our moral compasses can go haywire faster than you can say "I was just following orders."

Hurricane Katrina Disaster: Fast-forward to 2005, when Hurricane Katrina hit New Orleans. As floodwaters rose, so did the finger-pointing. Local officials waited for state help, state officials looked to the feds, and FEMA was probably trying to figure out their role in this disaster. The result? A game of bureaucratic hot potato that left over 1,800 dead and thousands stranded.

Financial Crisis of 2008: And let's revisit the 2008 financial crisis described earlier. It wasn't just about greedy bankers, although there were plenty of those. It was also about regulators, rating agencies, and risk managers all assuming someone else was minding the store. Spoiler alert number two: The store was on fire, and no one had bothered to check the smoke alarms.

Flint, Michigan, Public Health Debacle: Let's not forget Flint, Michigan. For eighteen months *after* officials learned that the city's tap water was toxic, residents unknowingly drank lead-contaminated water while bureaucrats at every level played a toxic game of "not it." It was like a government-wide version of that childhood game where the last one to touch their nose has to do the chores. Except in this case, the "chore" was protecting public health.

The lesson? When responsibility is diffused, accountability evaporates. It's like that group project in school where you ended up doing all the work while your teammates mastered the art of looking busy. The good news is there are ways to fight responsibility diffusion.

First, get specific. Vague goals are the breeding ground for "someone else will do it" syndrome. Instead of saying "We need to improve customer satisfaction," try "Janet, you're in charge of reducing wait times by 20 percent this quarter." Suddenly, Janet can't hide behind the collective "we" anymore.

Next, embrace the power of the spotlight. People act differently when they know they're being watched. We're not suggesting you install cameras in the break room. Instead, implement regular check-ins where team members report on their progress. It's amazing how much more gets done when people know they'll have to explain their (lack of) actions to the group.

Harness the motivational magic of peer pressure. Create a leaderboard or use public recognition for top performers.

Nothing lights a fire under someone quite like seeing their colleague get praised for doing the very thing they've been procrastinating on. You can also implement both individual and team-based rewards. This way, people are motivated to pull their own weight and make sure their teammates are doing the same. It's like turning your office into a friendly (but fierce) game of tug-of-war.

Lead by example. If you want your team to take ownership, show them how it's done. Admit your own mistakes, take on challenging tasks, and never utter the phrase "That's not my job."

> **MAVERICK PRO TIP**
>
> Unlock the 3-C Maverick Method by calling upon the team at a monthly status meeting to Catch which cognitive team distortion most often rears its ugly head. Address (as opposed to suppress) it so you can create a plan to Confront It and Change It.

Before you know it, you'll have created a culture where responsibility isn't diffused. It's embraced. By implementing these strategies, you can transform your team from a group of professional bystanders into a powerhouse of accountability. In the game of responsibility, the goal isn't to pass the buck. It's to score the touchdown.

When any of the four cognitive distortions takes hold of a team, everyone's confidence, motivation, and performance suffer. As a leader, it's your job to be an active listener, with your ears open and on alert for the language identified in the ten Monster behaviors that follow. These are strong indicators a problem is brewing:

Meeting team efforts with cynicism: People who dismiss the team's projects or efforts as pointless or doomed to fail.

Shooting down ideas: People who immediately respond to new ideas with "let me explain why that won't work," without giving them proper consideration.

Highlighting only the negative: People who focus exclusively on what's going wrong rather than acknowledging what's going right or the progress being made.

Undermining team decisions: People who express disagreement with team decisions in a way that erodes commitment and unity rather than one that embodies constructively voicing concerns during the decision-making process.

Withholding information: People who intentionally keep important information from other team members, which creates silos and prevents the team from functioning effectively.

Being passive-aggressive in communication: People who use sarcasm or backhanded compliments that can be hurtful and confusing, eroding trust among team members.

Resisting change: People who speak against any new initiatives or changes, regardless of their potential benefits, simply out of a desire to maintain the status quo.

Blaming others: People who consistently point fingers and refuse to be held accountable for challenges or failures.

Constantly complaining: People who frequently voice dissatisfaction about the team's direction, leadership, or other members without offering constructive feedback or solutions.

Gossiping: People who spread rumors or speak ill of team members behind their backs. This creates distrust and animosity within the team.

Headamentals: Team Derailer Assessment

This brief assessment will help you understand the extent to which members of your team display actions that negatively impact the team's effectiveness. It's a short list of statements that describe specific behaviors. Share this with your team and ask them to answer honestly.

Please consider how frequently people on your team exhibit each of the behaviors listed below—never, rarely, sometimes, often, or always—and assign each response the appropriate numerical value:

Never: 5
Rarely: 4
Sometimes: 3
Often: 2
Always: 1

Set aside ten minutes to complete this assessment in a quiet place. For the most accurate results, choose the first answer that comes to mind—and be honest.

People on our team:

1. Dismiss our efforts and projects as worthless or doomed to fail. _____

2. Shoot down ideas before anyone has a chance to consider them. _____

3. Focus only on what's going wrong rather than the progress being made. _____

4. Undermine team decisions and erode commitment to our decisions. _____

5   Intentionally keep important information from other team members.   _____

6   Use sarcasm or backhanded compliments that can be hurtful and shut down conversation.   _____

7   Speak against new initiatives or ideas.   _____

8   Consistently blame others and don't take responsibility for their errors.   _____

9   Constantly complain about things happening on our team without offering helpful suggestions.   _____

10 Spread rumors or gossip about people behind their backs.   _____

TOTAL   _____

Once everyone has completed the assessment, add up their scores. Here's how to interpret your results.

41–50 points: Your team is the model of a high-performing team. They are committed to their collective work and are looking ahead rather than back. They are operating in a psychologically safe environment, and this enables them to bring their best ideas forward without fear of criticism.

26–40 points: Your team has some level of trust in each other, but they're probably holding back a bit. Reinforce positive behaviors and call out negative team-talk and cognitive distortions as soon as you see them happening.

10–25 points: Your team is not aligned around a common purpose. They haven't really begun to trust each other yet so they're hesitant to share their ideas. It will take a focused effort for them to reach their potential.

These behaviors often stem from resistance to change or from stress or both. When a team displays even one of them, the behavior in question can quickly become a significant issue. Leaders must address these Monster tactics constructively and immediately to ensure a positive and collaborative environment.

Studies have shown that in a group setting, negative behaviors and attitudes can be up to five times more influential than positive ones, and a single negative team member can reduce group performance by 30 to 40 percent.

To mitigate these effects, leaders should address negative behaviors promptly, foster a positive team culture, and provide support for individuals who may be struggling with personal challenges that manifest as negativity in the workplace.

Here are some strategies for leaders to effectively interrupt negative, Monster team-talk:

Set clear expectations. Clearly communicate your expectations for positive and constructive communication within the team. Make sure each team member understands that negative talk is not aligned with the team's values and goals.

Lead by example. Through your behavior, demonstrate the kind of positive communication you expect from team members. Avoid participating in gripe sessions and focus instead on constructive and solution-oriented dialogue.

Address negative talk in the moment. When negative talk occurs, address it swiftly, politely, and firmly. You might say something like, "Let's focus on how we can solve this issue." Or, "I understand the frustration, but let's discuss possible solutions."

Encourage positive framing. Teach your team to reframe challenges as opportunities. Instead of focusing on what's going wrong, encourage discussions about what they learned and how they can help improve the situation.

17

Be the Change

When your values are clear to you, making decisions becomes easier.

ROY E. DISNEY

UP. THE INCREDIBLES. COCO. FINDING NEMO. It's been thirty years since Pixar Animation Studios set a new standard for animated films with the release of *Toy Story*. Since then, Pixar has consistently shattered boundaries and continued to innovate, creating films that speak to the inner child in all of us. In 2015, the studio released *Inside Out*, which brought us inside the mind of eleven-year-old Riley Andersen and introduced us to her self-talk roommates: Joy, Sadness, Anger, Fear, and Disgust. Her struggle to combat these emotional narratives was endearingly depicted and highly relatable to audiences young and old.

Pixar is a prime example of a company that has successfully implemented Headamentals strategies to build winning teams. The studio is well known for its creative excellence and has produced some of history's most beloved animated films. One of the critical factors behind Pixar's success is its commitment to fostering a culture of trust, candor, and open communication. This isn't just fancy talk for press releases; it's a key component of raising the bar to make better movies.

Ed Catmull, cofounder of Pixar, champions a culture of creativity where taking risks is encouraged and team members feel safe to share their thoughts openly. Pixar's "Braintrust" meetings are a cornerstone of its creative culture.

These meetings involve a group of directors and storytellers who come together to give candid feedback on a project. The environment is structured to be open and nonjudgmental, enabling honest feedback, and allowing for constructive criticism. This transparency helps creators improve their work without feeling attacked or demoralized.

Speaking about the meetings, Catmull says, "The Braintrust meets every few months or so to assess each movie we're making. Its premise is simple: put smart, passionate people in a room together, charge them with identifying and solving problems, and encourage them to be candid. The Braintrust is not foolproof, but when we get it right, the results are phenomenal."

Pixar also holds daily reviews where team members present their work and get immediate feedback. These sessions encourage continuous improvement and keep communication lines open. The emphasis is on collaborative problem-solving rather than criticism.

The leaders at Pixar lead by example, and they are consistent in their actions and with their words. They walk the talk because they are not afraid to talk the talk. They actively participate in the daily feedback sessions and are forthcoming about their own challenges and mistakes. This transparency has a trickle-down effect on team members, who are encouraged and inspired to be equally as transparent about their strengths and challenges.

While Suzy was earning her PhD in Social/Organizational Psychology at Columbia, she was a member of a "work group" that brought together all of the students who shared a dissertation advisor—one of the few required courses in the program. They met every week, and it was a wonderful opportunity for students to share their progress—developing their theory, completing their literature review, operationalizing their experiments, and analyzing their data. The feedback they received was honest, thoughtful, and always useful. Even when it was painful to recognize the holes in their work, together they enhanced the quality of everyone's research and provided a high level of moral support in a challenging environment that required everyone to bring their A game each and every day.

Walk the Talk: Values

Pixar's success is undoubtedly due to the strength of its carefully crafted culture, which is fueled by four guiding values: community, innovation, ownership, and authenticity. Each value reinforces the company's focus on creativity, collaboration, and making sure their people can operate within a productive and supportive environment.

The last thing the world needs is another leadership book about the importance of values, but if you find yourself wondering how to mold and shape positive team-talk, the answer is always, and without fail, values.

Patagonia is one of the best companies on the planet when it comes to walking the talk of its values. The company is known for its strong stance on environmental issues, actively participating in protective campaigns, supporting grassroots organizations, and even taking legal action to safeguard the environment. For the last forty years, Patagonia has committed 1 percent of total sales to the preservation and restoration of the environment, and any profit that is not reinvested in the company is used to fight the climate crisis. From environmentally friendly materials to supply chain transparency, Patagonia integrates these practices into its business model and clearly prioritizes sustainability above all (including fashion). The team-talk is aligned under the company's values, and each employee is committed to a unified, shared purpose. Everyone knows what to do and why they're doing it.

While Patagonia's values serve as a unifying force, values can also be used to effectively course correct unwanted behaviors. Agnelo Fernandes, CEO of Cote Hospitality in Minnesota, turns to his corporate values to squelch negative self-talk and to guide his team in a more productive direction. He says, "I have experienced situations where self-talk has exacerbated my company politics, enabling the cancer to spread, causing productivity to slow down, then to a halt, and eventually, we have abandoned innovation-driven projects because of one person—just one person (usually a narcissist in my experience)! I have no trick for this but to default to our core values, ICARE: Integrity, Compassion, Accountability, Respect, and Empowerment. I then let the person and team know that I am fully aware of the situation at hand and leverage our values to enable me to be fierce and courageous in doing the right thing."

When you are clear about your values, they serve as the ultimate touchstone for how your team operates in any situation. Clear values keep people focused on the shared goal, and they also keep people grounded when situations become unclear. They also prevent the angst that is often associated with tough decisions by eliminating uncertainty, and they have the added advantage of speeding up decision-making.

Slow It Down: Mindfulness

Throughout *Headamentals*, we've continually stressed the importance of picking up speed as a team. And yes, speed to ideation, speed to execution, and speed to decision-making are key components to success in the market. But often, the key to managing team-talk is taking the time to slow it all down, to make space in the day for mindful reflection.

As advisors to many leaders, we believe mindfulness is an important practice for teams to embark on together. The first formal investigation into the benefits of mindfulness in the Western world occurred in 1979 when Jon Kabat-Zinn developed the Mindfulness-Based Stress Reduction (MBSR) program at the University of Massachusetts Medical Center. Since then, an abundance of research into mindfulness has documented its myriad benefits, which are particularly helpful for those in leadership positions: improved mental health, better focus and concentration, greater creativity, stronger communication, and improved decision-making.

Practicing mindfulness in a team setting allows people to audit, address, and respond thoughtfully to situations, rather than react, fostering a more intentional collective style. It helps them maintain shared clarity and more effectively demonstrate genuine care and respect for others. It will also help you and everyone around you cultivate the presence, awareness, and compassion that are so essential for positive team-talk.

In the corporate world, where the pressure to perform is relentless, integrating mindfulness practices can be transformative. It's not hard to do, but it does require commitment, consistency, and patience. The good news is that mindfulness can be practiced live or virtually. All you need is a leader who is willing to devote a little time to being mindful.

Here are a few simple mindfulness techniques to get your team started:

- Set a specific time each week to consistently practice team mindfulness.

- Designate a quiet and comfortable place where people won't be disturbed. If virtual, ask people to turn off their cameras and mute their audio until they hear your voice.
- Ask the team to observe the rise and fall of their chests and the sensation of their breath entering and leaving their nostrils, chest, and abdomen.
- Remind them that when their mind wanders they should gently bring their focus back to their breath without judgment.
- Acknowledge that their judgy Monsters will try to take over, and that's OK. They are simply to notice and move on.
- Ask the team to pay attention to the thoughts that enter their minds and how their bodies are feeling.
- Ask them to experience the environment with all their senses.
- Continue the breathwork for five to ten minutes.

If you think mindfulness is a difficult habit to develop or a hokey practice to introduce to your team, kick that thought to the curb, and give mindfulness a chance. We've seen the effects a consistent mindfulness practice has on leaders and teams, and the proof is in the pudding.

Ten Headamentals Strategies for Productive Team-Talk

Culture change requires leaders who can positively impact team-talk. As Phil Jackson wisely observed, "You can't force your will on people. If you want them to act differently, you need to inspire them to change themselves."

We share here ten simple team-talk strategies to model Maverick behaviors in your organization. Some of them have been mentioned previously, and some are new. We're

Model the behaviors that healthy teams exhibit, and encourage team members to follow suit.

not asking you to use all ten every day, but if you pepper these practices into your team's work at appropriate intervals, they'll make a real difference.

1. Share the data about the impact of self-talk. Many teams aren't used to discussing topics like mental barriers, so talking about what you've learned about self-talk will help educate your team about the immutable connections between their thoughts and their performance. As we discussed in Chapter 8: "The Cognitive Reframe Game," cognitive behavioral therapy (CBT) is based on the idea that how you think about a situation impacts how you feel about it, which shapes how you act. Although you often can't control your reality, you can control how you think about it and how you behave in response.

2. Talk about real-life examples of business teams and athletes who have turned their performance around through positive self-talk. They'll serve as powerful motivators because through their example, the team will see the tangible benefits of developing a positive mindset.

3. Create safe spaces for dialogue. Promoting a culture where team members can openly discuss their thoughts without fear of judgment is essential for fostering positive teamtalk. Ensure team members feel safe expressing their ideas and concerns in team meetings, one-on-one sessions, and conversations at the watercooler. Make certain that everyone on your team, even the introverts, has a chance to voice their thoughts. These discussions help create an environment where people feel comfortable sharing and learning from each other.

4. Model the positive communication you want your team to use. By using positive language yourself, you'll set the

tone for your team and create a culture where positive team-talk is the norm.

5. Practice active listening. Quiet your thoughts to give your full attention to what your team is saying, and then remember what each individual is contributing to the conversation. This makes people feel heard and helps identify underlying issues that may need to be addressed.

6. Use our 3-C Maverick Method to redirect negative team-talk. As a refresher, here are the steps:

   Catch It: Recognize when you or members of your team are spiraling into destructive self-talk.

   Confront It: Encourage people to examine the source of the unproductive messages they're telling themselves and to confront them head-on to figure out if they're true.

   Change It: Help them generate alternative, more realistic narratives than the negative stories they've spent a lifetime perfecting.

7. Tailor strategies to employees' different needs. Each member of your team is unique. Use one-on-one conversations to learn about everyone's strengths and areas of self-doubt. Bake this into your regularly scheduled one-on-one conversations and work together to develop a plan to use positive self-talk to improve their performance.

8. Teach your team to be resilient in challenging situations. Normalizing a consistent mindfulness practice helps team members be more aware of their thought patterns. This will also help them stay calm and focused under pressure.

9. Incorporate team-talk in daily huddles. Start each huddle by sharing any success team members have had, no matter how small. Throw out daunting competitive scenarios

for them to solve, and make it fun! This will increase their mental agility and give them confidence when they need to adapt quickly and find solutions in real time.

10. Monitor the effectiveness of your team's team-talk strategies. Use team meetings and one-on-ones to gauge the extent to which your self-talk strategies are having a positive impact. Your team's success depends as much on having a strong, positive mindset as it does on their knowledge, skills, and abilities.

Headamentals: Team-Talk Check-In

Use the following quick assessment to check on the quality of your team's team-talk.

In a typical week, how often do team members display the following behaviors?

1. Talk about the impact of their self-talk _____
2. Share real-life examples of how positive team-talk is impacting their performance _____
3. Preserve the safe space you've created together _____
4. Model positive team-talk _____
5. Demonstrate active listening _____
6. Use our 3-C Maverick Method to redirect negative team-talk _____

7   Display resilience in the
    face of challenging situations   _____

8   Incorporate team-talk
    in daily huddles   _____

Like many things in life, more is better. In meetings and one-on-one conversations, model the behaviors that healthy teams exhibit, and encourage team members to follow suit. Talk about what's in it for them if the team can master positive team-talk.

And here's a bonus team-talk strategy: Gift *Headamentals* to your team members and fellow leaders so that they too can conquer their inner Monsters, retrain their brains, and step into their full Maverick potential.

Cultivating positive team-talk is *the* force differentiator plutonium for leaders. The Headamentals strategies for teams we've shared offer a comprehensive road map for cultivating a positive team culture anchored in a shared reality. Through practical activities such as providing a common vocabulary and keeping your ear to the ground for negative Monster saboteurs, you'll help your team develop and sustain positive Maverick-fed team-talk. Ultimately, the journey to high performance begins with the conversations we have with ourselves and each other, and leaders play a pivotal role in guiding these conversations in a positive direction. Team-talk starts at the top. Let *Headamentals* be your guide.

Speak to yourself with love and watch how your life transforms.

NIKKI ROWE

Conclusion
Celebrate Your Growth

NELSON MANDELA, South African anti-apartheid activist and the first president of South Africa, famously observed, "The greatest glory in living lies not in never falling but in rising every time you fall."

Many of the most important growth moments we have in life are seemingly invisible to everyone but ourselves. But learning to live in an inspired, determined Maverick state serves others too: When we serve ourselves well, we give others permission to serve themselves, and that should be celebrated.

When you complete a difficult task, overcome a fear, or reach a goal, don't just move on to the next task. Acknowledge what you've done. Create a snippet of space to tell yourself you did a good job. Life can be difficult, so don't cheat yourself out of a hard-earned pat on the back. Every achievement is worth celebrating! When you acknowledge a win or forgive yourself for messing up, that's the Maverick in you at work.

Self-talk isn't going away. Neither is your Monster. So, figure out which self-talk to embrace and which self-talk to shun. Your determined self knows where to look for productive messages while cutting off nourishment to the unproductive inner dialogue of your Monster. Trust your inner Maverick to create a new story for you. Give yourself grace when your Monster tries to spin you. In fact, thank your Monster.

In the end, our Monster is simply trying to keep us in the safe confines of whatever keeps us comfortable. But as we've all heard before, comfort is often the antithesis of growth. Find freedom in the power you have to live your life unencumbered by fears, opinions, or the falsehoods of others. They aren't yours. Each of us has the ability to lay down our mental swords and to use our inner stories as nourishment instead of a starvation regimen that works against us.

We wrote this book because we are committed to helping you grow. There is no change without courage and conflict. If you continue to remind yourself that growth comes from allowing yourself to be uncomfortable, you'll be better able to handle whatever life throws your way, and you can become kinder to yourself and others. Our hope is that we have given you the tools to put yourself on the path to becoming the person you were always meant to be. The world needs you, and it's waiting for you.

A Word of Caution

WHILE WE know this book is filled with wisdom and practical tools to master the Monster in your mind, practicing the behaviors we've just talked about is not a substitute treatment if you're experiencing suicidal thoughts, PTSD, or severe trauma.

More than fifty thousand people in the United States took their own lives in 2023, the highest number ever, according to a study posted recently by the Centers for Disease Control and Prevention (CDC). And the numbers are climbing. The suicide rate in 2022 was 4 percent higher than it was in 2021, and that was a 3 percent increase from the year before. Stressful life events such as financial and legal challenges and real-world factors such as shame, harassment, bullying, discrimination, and relationship troubles may contribute to suicide risk.

If you or someone you know is at risk of suicide because of unrelenting negative thoughts, there are many avenues of support. Here are a few:

- The US National Suicide Prevention Lifeline: Phone 1-800-273-TALK (1-800-273-8255) or visit online (https://suicidepreventionlifeline.org/).

- The 988 Suicide & Crisis Lifeline: Call or text 988 (para ayuda en español, llame al 988). The Lifeline provides free confidential support to anyone in suicidal crisis or emotional distress twenty-four hours a day, seven days a week.
- Call 911 in life-threatening situations.

Also consider reaching out to the following support lines:

- Crisis Text Line (USA): Text HOME to 741741 or visit online (crisistextline.org).
- Veterans Crisis Line (USA): Phone 1-800-273-8255 (Press 1), text 838255, or visit online (veteranscrisisline.net).
- International Suicide Hotlines: If you're not in the US, there are numerous suicide prevention hotlines worldwide.
- Local Crisis Centers and Hotlines: Search for crisis centers or hotlines in your local area, as there may be specific resources available to you.
- Therapy and Counseling Services: Seek help from a mental health professional or therapist who can provide long-term support and treatment for mental health issues.
- Don't hesitate to reach out to friends and family members for support. Sometimes, talking to someone you trust can make a significant difference.

Acknowledgments

THANK YOU. Thank you. And, also, thank you.

When three authors come together, one thank you is never enough.

First, a thank you to the Monster in our minds. For it is both a blessing and a curse learning to live with you as our roommate. Without you, there is no three-year project. To acknowledge you, Monster, is to admit that while you are as ordinary as the air we breathe, you remained the belle of this book who took serious energy and detective work to understand. The authors have come to respect you. Without you, there would be no need for *Headamentals*.

Second, the authors wish to thank our "entourage of excellence," composed of many early readers who shared their ideas, challenged us to delve deeper, and appropriately pushed us to go for more. All of you became the glue who helped us stick the landing on an arena of concepts, ideas, and stories that now make up what's in your hands (and on your screens).

A huge shout-out to the wonderfully wise Dr. Nicholas Alp, who helped us make sense of this complex organ of a brain that rules our thoughts. The authors want to extend gratitude and a cap tip to the brilliant clinical behavior analyst Gianna Biscontini, who remains the godmother of the term *mental junk food.* You brought science and soul to the early days of this scene for the collective betterment, as you would say, of the book. We'd also be remiss if we didn't give a shout-out to Yenie Caballero, who got us thinking about calling our negative self-talk a Monster. A light went off, and this became the metaphor we used throughout the book.

To the full team at Page Two—but especially Brooke White, who used her wit and wizardry to weave together a tight storyline that makes this comprehensive book worth reading. To designer Cameron McKague and creative director Peter Cocking, the brains behind the egg image on our cover. Yes, we are fragile creatures—each doing our best to "crack" our self-talk. To Tass Barry, for keeping us on track while putting up with us; to Viktoria Skaper, for her sharp marketing mind; to Felicia Quon, the true savant of sales; and finally, to the two fantastic founders of Page Two, Jesse Finkelstein and Trena White, for believing in our project.

Finally, each of the three authors would like to thank "their people."

Suzy would like to extend her heartfelt gratitude to the social psychologists whose groundbreaking research has profoundly shaped our understanding of human behavior. Their dedication to unraveling the complexities of social interactions has provided invaluable insights into our understanding of how we can tame our Monsters and live richer, more fulfilling lives. Suzy also wants to thank her husband for being an enthusiastic first reader and always supportive of her work.

Ryan sends all the love in the world to his brave wife, who went back to school, while juggling two kids under the age of ten, to become a therapist. The world will be brighter and better because of the impact you will undoubtedly make. To Ryan's parents and to those two kids Ryan *gets* to parent, you embody all the reasons why Ryan does what he does. Ryan would also like to thank his partners at Courageous—Billy, Nicole, and Kimberly—who are almost always on the same "wavelength"; each gave him the grace and space to nudge *Headamentals* over the finish line.

Rhett wants to thank his family for giving him the space and support to follow his passions. He sends a shout-out to his mentors and coaches for their invaluable guidance. And a special thank you to those who doubted him; you strengthened Rhett and taught him the value of healthy self-talk. His family's belief, encouragement, and challenges have shaped this journey, and Rhett is deeply grateful for that.

Thanks to our early readers, who provided the insightful feedback that we happily incorporated in the book:

Maureen Breeze, author, choreographer
Terry Brown, strategy consultant, entrepreneur
Ed Burke, American businessman, entrepreneur
Joyel Crawford, keynote speaker, author
Jenifer Farrell, Vice President, Information Technology, NPCC
Hyvron Jean, Vice President, Technology, UPO
Colonel Tony "Ripper" Nerad, USMC (Ret.), Harrier Jet Pilot
Michael Notardonato, actor, entrepreneur
John Reed, executive coach, author
Margaux Swaby, leader, change agent
Christine Woodside, author, journalist

References

Beck, Aaron. *Cognitive Therapy and the Emotional Disorders.* Plume, 1979.

Berman, Ryan. *Return on Courage: A Business Playbook for Courageous Change.* Greenleaf Book Group Press, 2019.

Breeze, Maureen, and Suzanne Schimmel. *Playing the Long Game: A Handbook for Parenting Elite and College Athletes.* Independently published, 2022.

Burnett, Bill. "5 Steps to Designing the Life You Want." TEDx Talk, April 2017, Stanford. Video, 25 min., 20 sec. https://www.youtube.com/watch?v=SemHh0n19LA.

Catmull, Ed. "Inside the Pixar Braintrust." *Fast Company*, March 12, 2014. https://www.fastcompany.com/3027135/inside-the-pixar-braintrust.

Clance, Pauline Rose, and Suzanne Ament Imes. "The Imposter Phenomenon in High Achieving Women: Dynamics and Therapeutic Intervention." *Psychotherapy: Theory, Research & Practice* 15, no. 3 (1978): 241–247. https://doi.org/10.1037/h0086006.

Crist, Carolyn. "Loneliness Is Severely Affecting Employees at Work, Study Shows." HR Dive, November 17, 2023. https://www.hrdive.com/news/loneliness-high-levels-employees-work-new-study-shows/700131/.

Darley, John M., and Bibb Latané. "Bystander Intervention in Emergencies: Diffusion of Responsibility." *Journal of Personality and Social Psychology* 8, no. 4 (1968): 377–383. https://doi.org/10.1037/h0025589.

Davlembayeva, Dinara, and Savvas Papagiannidis. "Social Influence Theory: A Review." In *TheoryHub Book*, edited by Savvas Papagiannidis. TheoryHub, 2024. https://open.ncl.ac.uk/theory-library/social-influence-theory.pdf.

Dweck, Carol. *Mindset: The New Psychology of Success*. Ballantine Books, 2007.

Dweck, Carol. "The Power of Believing That You Can Improve." TED Talk, November 2014, Norrköping. Video, 10 min., 10 sec. https://www.ted.com/talks/carol_dweck_the_power_of_believing_that_you_can_improve.

Felps, Will, Terence R. Mitchell, and Eliza Byington. "How, When, and Why Bad Apples Spoil the Barrel: Negative Group Members and Dysfunctional Groups." *Research in Organizational Behavior* 27, no. 3 (2006): 175–222. https://doi.org/10.1016/S0191-3085(06)27005-9.

Festinger, Leon. *A Theory of Cognitive Dissonance*. Stanford University Press, 1957.

Godin, Seth. "Keynote Speech." Digital Summit, Denver, Colorado, June 27–28, 2017.

Goldsmith, Marshall, and Mark Reiter. *Triggers: Creating Behavior That Lasts, Becoming the Person You Want to Be*. Crown Business, 2015.

Goldsmith, Marshall, with Mark Reiter. *What Got You Here Won't Get You There: How Successful People Become Even More Successful!* Hachette Books, 2007.

Goleman, Daniel. *Emotional Intelligence: Why It Can Matter More Than IQ*. Bantam, 1995.

Haney, Craig, Curtis Banks, and Philip Zimbardo. "Interpersonal Dynamics in a Simulated Prison." *International Journal of Criminology and Penology* 1 (1973): 69–97. http://pdf.prisonexp.org/ijcp1973.pdf.

Hastings, Reed, and Erin Meyer. *No Rules Rules: Netflix and the Culture of Reinvention*. Penguin Press, 2020.

Jackson, Phil, and Hugh Delehanty. *Eleven Rings: The Soul of Success*. Penguin Books, 2014.

Janis, Irving L. *Victims of Groupthink: A Psychological Study of Foreign-Policy Decisions and Fiascoes*, second edition. Houghton Mifflin, 1982 (1972).

Jones, Edward E., and Steven Berglas. "Control of Attributions about the Self through Self-Handicapping Strategies: The Appeal of Alcohol and the Role of Underachievement." *Personality and Social Psychology Bulletin* 4, no. 2 (1978): 200–206. https://doi.org/10.1177/014616727800400205.

Kassem, Suzy. *Rise Up and Salute the Sun: The Writings of Suzy Kassem*. Awakened Press, 2011.

Kross, Ethan, Emma Bruehlman-Senecal, Jiyoung Park, et al. "Self-Talk as a Regulatory Mechanism: How You Do It Matters." *Journal of Personality and Social Psychology* 106, no. 2 (2014): 304–324. https://doi.org/10.1037/a0035173.

Lally, Phillippa, Cornelia H. M. van Jaarsveld, Henry W. W. Potts, and Jane Wardle. "How Are Habits Formed: Modelling Habit Formation in the Real World." *European Journal of Social Psychology* 40, no. 6 (2010): 998–1009. https://doi.org/10.1002/ejsp.674.

Leadership Skills. "Rethinking Imposter Syndrome (and How to Overcome It!)." Lead Bee, Leadership Development. https://leadbeeleadership.com/leadership-skills/imposter-syndrome/.

Lewis, Abbey. "New to Leadership? Here's How to Address Loneliness." Harvard Business Publishing (blog), February 3, 2023. https://www.harvardbusiness.org/new-to-leadership-heres-how-to-address-loneliness/.

Lewis, Neil A. "On a Supreme Court Prospect's Resumé: 'Baseball Savior.'" *The New York Times*, May 14, 2009. https://www.nytimes.com/2009/05/15/us/15sotomayor.html.

Miller, George A. "The Magical Number Seven, Plus or Minus Two: Some Limits on Our Capacity for Processing Information." *Psychological Review* 63 (1956): 81–97. https://doi.org/10.1037/h0043158.

Nasher, Jack. "The Imposter Phenomenon: Why the Best Feel Like Frauds." *Forbes*, December 3, 2018. https://www.forbes.com/sites/jacknasher/2018/12/03/the-imposter-phenomenon-and-two-more-reasons-why-the-best-feel-like-frauds/.

Noble, David, and Carol Kauffman. *Real-Time Leadership: Find Your Winning Moves When the Stakes Are High*. Harvard Business Review Press, 2023.

Nolen-Hoeksema, Susan. *Women Who Think Too Much: How to Break Free of Overthinking and Reclaim Your Life*. Henry Holt and Company, 2003.

NPR. "Tom Hanks Says Self-Doubt Is 'A High-Wire Act That We All Walk.'" *Fresh Air*. April 26, 2018. https://www.npr.org/2016/04/26/475573489/tom-hanks-says-self-doubt-is-a-high-wire-act-that-we-all-walk.

Office of the US Surgeon General. *Our Epidemic of Loneliness and Isolation: The US Surgeon General's Advisory on the Healing Effects of Social Connection and Community*. US Department of Health and

Human Services. 2023. https://www.hhs.gov/sites/default/files/surgeon-general-social-connection-advisory.pdf.

Poler, Michelle. *Hello, Fears: Crush Your Comfort Zone and Become Who You're Meant to Be*. Sourcebooks, 2020.

Rock, Chris. *Chris Rock: Selective Outrage*. Netflix, 2023. 70 min.

Sakulku, Jaruwan, and James Alexander. "The Impostor Phenomenon." *International Journal of Behavioral Science* 6, no. 1 (2011): 73–92. https://doi.org/10.14456/ijbs.2011.6.

Sandberg, Sheryl. *Lean In: Women, Work, and the Will to Lead*. Alfred A. Knopf, 2013.

Simone, Fran. "Negative Self-Talk: Don't Let It Overwhelm You." *Psychology Today*, December 4, 2017. https://www.psychologytoday.com/ca/blog/family-affair/201712/negative-self-talk-dont-let-it-overwhelm-you.

Smith, Lydia. "Why Women Experience 'Impostor Syndrome'—and How to Beat It." *Cosmopolitan*, August 18, 2017. https://www.cosmopolitan.com/uk/reports/a12029501impostor-syndrome-women-what-is-it-how-to-beat-it/.

Stansfield, Sandy. "Mental Well-Being in Coaching: Insights, Strategies, and Practical Takeaways." International Coaching Federation (blog), November 21, 2024. https://coachingfederation.org/blog/mental-well-being-in-coaching-insights-strategies-and-practical-takeaways.

Staw, Barry M. "Knee-Deep in the Big Muddy: A Study of Escalating Commitment to a Chosen Course of Action." *Organizational Behavior & Human Performance* 16, no. 1 (1976): 27–44. https://doi.org/10.1016/0030-5073(76)90005-2.

US Bureau of Labor Statistics. "American Time Use Survey News Release." United States Department of Labor Economic News Release, July 22, 2021. https://www.bls.gov/news.release/archives/atus_07222021.htm.

US Bureau of Labor Statistics. "Time Spent Alone Increased by an Hour Per Day in 2020." TED: The Economics Daily, August 27, 2021. https://www.bls.gov/opub/ted/2021/time-spent-alone-increased-by-an-hour-per-day-in-2020.htm.

Voss, Chris, with Tahl Raz. *Never Split the Difference: Negotiating as if Your Life Depended on It*. Harper Business, 2016.

Wells, Ellory. "Leadership Principles from Legendary Basketball Coach Phil Jackson." Ellory Wells (blog), December 5, 2013. https://www.ellorywells.com/leadership-principles-phil-jackson/.

About the Authors

Suzy Burke, PhD, president and cofounder of Accountability Inc., is a seasoned executive with an exceptional track record in a diverse array of businesses, from a Fortune 20 technology company to a highly successful beverage start-up. She grounds her work in a deep understanding of human behavior as well as a research-based knowledge of what it takes to create vibrant, values-based, accountable cultures that maximize the potential of each individual. A social/organizational psychologist, she is a National Institute of Mental Health scholar, a member of the renowned Marshall Goldsmith 100 Coaches Agency, and a highly regarded executive advisor.

Ryan Berman is a corporate fear fighter. He's the founder of Courageous, the author of *Return on Courage*, and the host of *The Courageous Podcast*. For over twenty-five years, Ryan has helped corporations that have been stuck, scared, stale, or safe choose courage. He has counseled on the topic at many companies, including Google, Procter & Gamble, Kellogg's, Kraft Heinz, Bausch + Lomb, Atlanta Falcons, Houston Texans, LA Galaxy, and Snapchat. His consulting firm, Courageous, is a full-spectrum courage company, guiding its clients through courageous conversations, courageous decisions, courageous ideas, and courageous transformations. Ryan believes that change is hard, but the hardships that come from not changing are far harder.

Rhett Power is the CEO and cofounder of the leadership consultancy Accountability Inc. He helps leaders and entrepreneurs break free from limitations, embrace bold decisions, and navigate organizational growth. Named the #1 Thought Leader on Entrepreneurship by Thinkers360 and a top Startup and Management Thinker by Global Gurus, Rhett is also a Marshall Goldsmith 100 Coach. His bestselling *Entrepreneur's Book of Actions* provides actionable insights for leaders, and his expertise has been featured in *Forbes*, *Inc.*, *Fast Company*, *Wall Street Journal*, on CNBC, and more. Rhett also co-hosts *Best Seller Live* on Apple TV.

How to Find Us

We welcome you to see for yourself that you're not alone. If you need a little nudge, and you value community, you can head to our website and join our private Headamentals group (headamentals.com/mavericks).